Contract Law in Israel

Contract Law in Israel

Second Edition

Gabriela Shalev

This book was originally published as a monograph in the International Encyclopaedia of Laws/Contracts.

Founding Editor: Roger Blanpain
General Editor: Frank Hendrickx
Volume Editor: Jacques Herbots

Wolters Kluwer

Published by:
Kluwer Law International B.V.
PO Box 316
2400 AH Alphen aan den Rijn
The Netherlands
E-mail: international-sales@wolterskluwer.com
Website: lrus.wolterskluwer.com

Sold and distributed by:
Wolters Kluwer Legal & Regulatory U.S.
7201 McKinney Circle
Frederick, MD 21704
United States of America
Email: customer.service@wolterskluwer.com

ISBN 978-94-035-2990-5

e-Book: ISBN 978-94-035-2925-7
web-PDF: ISBN 978-94-035-2930-1

The Author

Prof. Gabriela Shalev is a Professor of Law (Emeritus) at the Hebrew University in Jerusalem and a senior faculty member at the Ono Academic College in Israel. In 2010, Prof. Shalev completed a two-year term as Israel's Ambassador to the United Nations, the first woman in Israel to hold this position. Since returning to Israel Prof. Shalev has joined several academic councils and public bodies and has been appointed for a second three-year term to the Board of Directors of Bank Leumi Le-Israel Ltd. She served twice (2012 and 2013) as the Head of the Sapir Prize Committee (the Israeli Booker Prize).

Shalev taught, as a Guest Professor, Contract Law and Comparative Law in universities in North America, Europe and Canada. She is a permanent participant in international conferences as an expert on contract law and comparative law. For many years, Shalev was the Chief Editor of the Israel Supreme Court judgments and editor of the legal section of the Hebrew Encyclopedia. She is a member of the International Academy of Comparative Law.

Shalev received the Susman Law Prize (1989), the Zeltner Law Prize (1991), and in 2003 she won an honorary prize of the Israeli Bar Association for special achievements in academic research. In 2010 she received the Dr Bernard Heller Prize from the Hebrew Union College and the Distinguished Leadership Award from the American Jewish Committee.

Shalev published thirteen books and over 100 articles, most of them dealing with Contract Law and Comparative Law. Her books on Contract Law are used as the basic books on the subject throughout Israel.

Shalev is a leading world expert on the subjects of Contract Law and Procurement Contracts. In addition to her academic work, she provides expert legal advice and expert legal opinions to public bodies, institutions, arbitrators and lawyers, in Israel and abroad.

Prior to her term in the United Nations, she was a member of many public bodies and committees (among them Acting Chairman of the Israel Broadcasting Authority, member of the Jewish Agency Board of Governors, member of the Tribunal for Standard Form Contracts, member of the Committee for Codification of Civil Law, member of the Executive of the Israeli Democracy Institute, and a member of

The Author

Boards of Directors of leading Israeli companies (Israel Electric Company, Teva Pharmaceuticals Industry, Osem Investments, Delek Ltd.)).

This monograph was written with the assistance of, Shira Gur-Arieh, a fourth year law student at Hebrew University and Professor Shalev's research assistant. Shira began her clerkship in September 2020 at the Supreme Court.

Table of Contents

Preface

This monograph is based on Professor Gabriela Shalev's books (in Hebrew): *The Law of Contract*,[1] *The Law of Contract – Remedies for Breach*[2] and *The Law of Public Procurement*.[3]

The subjects described in this monograph generally correspond with similar subjects discussed in depth in the above-mentioned books. Hence, as a general note, for further discussion of any topic in this monograph, please see the parallel chapter in the above-mentioned books.

1. Gabriela Shalev & Efi Zemach, *The Law of Contract* (4th ed. 2019).
2. Gabriela Shalev & Yehuda Adar, *The Law of Contract – Remedies for Breach* (2009).
3. Gabriela Shalev, *The Law of Public Procurement* (1999).

General Introduction

§1. THE GENERAL BACKGROUND OF THE COUNTRY

I. Geography

1. The State of Israel is a small country, located in the Asian part of the Middle East. It covers an area of 22,145 sq. km, and has a land frontier with Egypt (South), Jordan (East), Lebanon and Syria (North), and a coastline along the Mediterranean Sea (West). It has a population of approximately 9,136,000 inhabitants as of December 2019.

II. History

2. The State of Israel was established on 14 May 1948. Before the establishment of the State, the area had been part of the Ottoman Empire since the sixteenth century until the end of the First World War and the British occupation of the Middle East. According to a decision of the League of Nations, the area (known then as 'Palestine') became a British Mandate, a status which lasted until 1948. According to a resolution of 29 November 1947, the UN declared that Palestine would be divided into two independent states: a Jewish state and an Arab state. Subsequently, the British evacuated Palestine. The Arab states, refusing to acknowledge the UN Resolution, declared war against the would-be State of Israel and the Jewish inhabitants. In the midst of that war, known as the 'War of Independence', the State of Israel was established. As a result of the Arab world's continuous refusal to acknowledge the existence of the State of Israel, frequent wars and acts of terrorism have besieged the area. This state of affairs was partially altered following the signing of a peace treaty between Israel and Egypt in 1979. Since 1987 the 'uprising' ('intifada') in the areas occupied by Israel following the 1967 Six Day War has caused new tension and turmoil in relations between Jewish and Arab people in Israel. Following the Madrid Convention, which took place in October 1991, Israel and the Hashemite Kingdom of Jordan signed a peace treaty in October 1994. Following secret negotiations, which took place in Oslo, Israel and the Palestinian Liberation Organization, signed a series of documents. The most important of these documents are the Declaration of Principles on Interim Self-Government Arrangements signed in Washington in September 1993, the Agreement on the Gaza Strip and Jericho Area signed in Cairo in May 1994 and the Agreement on Interim Self-Government Arrangements signed in Washington in October 1995. All those together with the establishment of diplomatic relations with other Arab countries and the peace negotiations, which are being held with neighbouring Syria, raise new hopes for a comprehensive peaceful solution of the Middle East conflict.

III. The People

3. The State of Israel was established as a national homeland for the Jewish people, which had been scattered throughout the Diaspora. The ambition to create such a homeland is an important component of the national identity of the State of Israel and was explicitly pronounced in the State's Declaration of Independence. The population, therefore, is composed mainly of Jews, who immigrated to Israel from various countries around the world. About half of the Jewish population are immigrants from Arab and Asian countries, who fled from those countries after 1948, or their descendants. The other halves are Jews from American, European and East European countries, many of whom are survivors of the Holocaust. Since 1990, approximately 1,200,000 Russians immigrated to Israel when the USSR borders opened. This adds to the Jewish population, composed of inhabitants from various cultural backgrounds.

4. As of December 2019, the Israeli population comprised 9,136,000 inhabitants: 6,772,000 Jews, 1,916,000 Moslems and 448,000 other small minorities, including Christians and Druze.

IV. Language

5. Israel has two official languages: Hebrew (mainly spoken by the Jewish inhabitants) and Arabic (mainly spoken by other minorities).

V. The Political System

6. The State of Israel has a democratic-republican regime, which is based upon the constitutional principles of the self-government of the people, the separation of powers, the rule of law and human rights.

VI. The Presidency

7. The President of Israel is a figurehead and the representative of the State, whose roles are mainly symbolic and ceremonial. The President signs the laws made by the Knesset (the Israeli Parliament) and accepts the credentials of foreign diplomats. In addition to these ceremonial duties the President has two discretionary powers: to grant presidential amnesty and to choose the Knesset member who may form the new government after elections have taken place. The President is elected by the Knesset, and may serve for a single seven-year term.

VII. The Knesset

8. The Knesset is the highest legislative authority in Israel. In the absence of a written constitution, the Knesset has almost unlimited legislative authority. However, the Knesset also has a role as the framer of the future Israeli Constitution. In this capacity, the Knesset has enacted a series of statutes concerning constitutional issues, known as the basic laws, dealing with the authorities of the Knesset, the government, the judiciary, the army and the presidency. When this work is completed, the basic laws will form the Israeli Constitution. Accordingly, some of the basic laws impose constraints on the unlimited authority of the Knesset, in that only a special majority of all Knesset members can alter them.

9. According to the Basic Law: the Knesset, the Knesset is elected by a secret ballot in direct, equal and proportional elections, and the entire state is considered one electoral district. The Knesset is elected for a four-year term; although in the last three decades, no Knesset completed its full term. Every citizen over 18 years may vote in the elections and may be elected when he or she reaches the age of 21 (with the exception of judges, high officials and the President, who cannot be elected to the Knesset). The Knesset has 120 members belonging to about ten different political parties.

VIII. The Government

10. The Government is the executive authority, and the Prime Minister, being the head of the Government, is the highest executive authority. The Government is composed of members of the Knesset and members of the various political parties, which form the dominant coalition group within the Knesset (no political party ever achieved an absolute majority that would enable it to form the Government by itself). The Government must gain the confidence of the Knesset for its actions. After elections and the formation of the Government, the Knesset must cast a vote of confidence in the Government. During its four-year term, the Knesset may vote for no-confidence in the Government, forcing a new Government to be composed. The powers of the Government are granted in the Basic Law: the Government.

IX. The Judiciary

11. The judiciary in Israel consists of the regular courts as well as various special courts. The regular court system is composed of a hierarchy of three courts: the Magistrates' Court (a Court of First Instance for minor civil and criminal cases), the District Court (a Court of First Instance for major cases and an appellate tribunal over the Magistrates' Court) and the Supreme Court (an appellate tribunal over the District Courts). The Supreme Court also serves as the 'High Court of Justice', dealing with administrative and constitutional issues, involving complaints against the State's authorities.

12. A separate tribunal is the Labour Courts, dealing with labour law and social security law, as an independent instance. The Labour Court is composed of a two-level hierarchy – the Regional Courts (the first instance) and the National Court (the appellate instance).

13. Another separate system consists of the various religious courts, dealing with matters of personal status and belonging to the different religious communities living in Israel: the Rabbinical Courts (for Jews), the Sharia Courts (for Moslems and Druze) and Ecclesial Courts (for the different Christian communities).

14. The judges are elected by secret ballot by a committee composed of members of the Knesset, ministers, judges and members of the Israeli bar.

§2. Israeli Law as a Mixed Jurisdiction

15. The Israeli legal system in general and Israeli contract law in particular cannot be categorized as part of one unified legal family, e.g., common law or civil law. Instead, the Israeli legal system is uniquely constituted by different 'legal layers' and may be described as a system of 'mixed jurisdiction'.

16. Until the end of the First World War, Palestine, including the area of present-day Israel, formed part of the Ottoman Empire. Turkish rule was followed by British rule, which lasted until the establishment of the State of Israel on 14 May 1948. The different rulers of Palestine prescribed various legal systems, so that the law on the eve of independence was composed of various legal systems based on different sources, mainly Ottoman and British. The Ottoman law which applied in Palestine was mainly the Mejelle, a codification which was continentally oriented, and at the same time, influenced by Islamic law. The British law, which applied in Palestine, was mainly common law and equity.

17. At first, the new State of Israel, seeking to avoid disruption of the social fabric in the wake of political change, preserved the existing legal order by prescribing the legal norms created by the former rulers. In the initial years of statehood, Israeli legislation consisted mostly of amendments in certain areas where this was considered particularly urgent. Only during the last five decades has the legislature become more active, mainly in the area of private law.

18. After the enactment of initial Israeli legislation, Israeli law entered a transitional stage. During this period, English common law, as well as the Mejelle, remained in force, and applied to contracts created before the new enactments, while new original Israeli legislation, based on various sources, gradually took their place. During the ensuing years, the number of contracts subject to the previous law steadily decreased.

19. Yet, even after this transitional stage, Israeli contract law is still a mixed jurisdiction. The legislation in the field of contract law is based on civil law, common law and Jewish law. This co-existence of different institutions, adopted from different legal families, accords Israeli private law the title of a mixed jurisdiction. The Contract (General Part) Law, 1973, was enacted in the Israeli legal system over forty years ago and is part of a comprehensive uniform legislative framework of civil law, which created a legal revolution in contract law in Israel. As a result, contract law transformed into an original and independent structured set of laws, placing emphasis on the provisions of the law rather than case law. However, in this transitional stage, jurists were required to apply both old and new laws, in regard to contracts performed prior to the enactment of the Contract (General Part) Law, 1973. At present, there is almost no need to refer to the old law.

20. In the last four decades there has been an attempt to incorporate and consolidate a multitude of various laws in the area of private law into a uniform legislative framework: a civil code resembling European codifications such as the French Code Civil, the German B.G.B. and the Italian Codice Civile. These efforts, which began in the 1980s with the formation of the Codification Committee, presided by Former Chief Justice Aharon Barak, have yet to bear fruit. Although a bill, incorporating the suggested Code, was drafted by the Knesset in 2011, it seems now that the bill will not become effective in the near future.

21. At present, three main statues govern Israeli contract law: The Contracts (General Part) Law, 1973 (hereinafter: General Contracts Law or Contracts); the Contracts (Remedies for Breach of Contract) Law, 1970 (hereinafter: the Remedies Law), and the Standard Contracts Law, 1982. The General Contracts Law lays the fundamental principles that govern contractual relationships; it covers topics such as the formation of the contract, its validity, content and conditions. This Law was meant to serve as the basis of the forthcoming codification. The Remedies Law provides the basis for awarding remedies in contractual disputes. The provisions of the Remedies Law reflect a mixture of civil and common law approaches to remedies for breach of contracts. The aim of the Standard Contracts Law is to protect customers against unduly disadvantageous conditions in standard contracts.[1]

§3. Primacy of Legislation

22. The Israeli legal system is based on the notion of the primacy of legislation over all other sources of law (such as case law or customary law). In the absence of

1. For further discussion (in English) regarding the three above-mentioned statues, *see* Gabriela Shalev, *General Comments on Contracts (General Part) Law, 1973*, 9 Isr. Law. Rev. 274 (1974); Yehuda Adar & Gabriela Shalev, *The Law of Remedies in a Mixed Jurisdiction: The Israeli Experience*, 23 Tul. Eur. & Civ. L.F. 111 (2008); Gabriela Shalev, *Standard Contracts under Israeli Law*, 10 Tel Aviv U. Stud. Law. 229 (1990).

a written constitution, the primacy of legislation is a basic factor in the Israeli constitutional system. Even so, some important areas of the legal system are still based on case law, which was the main source of contract law during the first years of statehood.

§4. The Position of the Judiciary

23. From the early 1960s a dramatic change in the distribution of functions between the legislature and the judiciary has taken place in the field of contract law. Whereas in the past, during the period of the formal and substantive rule of English law over contract law, the judges had been accorded pre-eminence in the application and implementation of the law, at present, the task of the judges has become secondary to that of the legislature. While the legislature establishes the contractual provisions of the substantive law, the role of the judges is primarily to apply and implement the legislative innovations. Yet, since the legislation contains many broad expressions that constitute legal standards or prototypes of behaviour, a wide margin has been left open for judicial law-making. The development of important doctrines, such as good faith, public policy, and unjust enforcement, is left in the hands of the judiciary, which is responsible for giving a practical meaning to these statutory standards. As new problems emerge that were unanticipated by the legislator, the courts creatively use their powers to formulate new doctrines, by way of judicial legislation. An interesting example of such judicial creations is the rules concerning the adjustment of the contractual price during periods of high inflation.[2]

§5. Distinction Between Public Law and Private Law

24. The distinction between public law and private law is based on the notion that public law includes all legal fields involving important public interests, protected by the state. The field of public law traditionally includes penal law, tax law, administrative law and constitutional law. Today public law also includes various social security laws. Private law, however, comprises all legal fields, concerning the various legal relationships, which may exist between citizens in the various areas of private and economic life. This category includes contract law, property law, succession law, tort law and commercial law.

25. In 1992, the Knesset enacted two new basic laws: *Basic Law: Human Dignity and Liberty* and *Basic Law: Freedom of Occupation.* This new constitutional reality raised the question of the applicability of these basic laws to private law in general, and to contract law in particular. In some decisions of the Supreme Court Chief Justice Barak expressed his view that constitutional rights apply not only to public law but to private law as well, though in an indirect manner. These basic laws flow into private law *via* the established channels of private law, such as good faith

2. For further discussion, *see* para. 80.

and public policy. Thus, in Barak's view, the implementation of civil rights is not the duty of the state only; the basic laws are also applicable in relations among private individuals.

26. The enactment of the Prohibition of Discrimination Law, 2000, which imposed a duty of equality on some private actors, has further blurred the lines of demarcation between public and private law.[3] Although the law does not relate strictly to contract law, as it defines the prohibited discrimination as a tort, it does address the pre-contractual stage.[4]

§6. DISTINCTION BETWEEN CIVIL LAW AND COMMERCIAL LAW

27. In theory, commercial law deals with the special aspects of various kinds of corporate bodies, such as corporations and partnerships, as well as with the securities market. In practice, most of commercial law is based on contract law, agency law and property law. Commercial law and civil law are both litigated in the civil courts.

3. *See* Prohibition of Discrimination in Products, Services, and Entry into Places of Entertainment and Public Places Law, 5761-2000.
4. For further discussion, *see* para. 163.

Introduction to the Law of Contracts

§1. Definition of a Contract

28. The General Contracts Law, which is the basic and most important piece of legislation in the area of contracts, does not include a definition of the term 'contract', although this term is used extensively throughout the law. A contract in Israeli law may be defined as an enforceable agreement. This definition contains two elements: agreement and enforceability.

29. The first element of the definition of the term 'contract' is agreement. This element indicates that a contract is based on the agreement of the parties. This agreement is the outcome of the parties' wills. A contract reflects the meeting of wills (meeting of the minds) or a *consensus.*

30. However, a mere agreement is not sufficient. For the element of agreement to exist, the parties' agreement must be conscious and aimed at making a binding legal contract.

31. In modern commercial and economic life there are many factual situations where no real agreement exists, but a contract is nonetheless formed. Such situations may occur when one party finds itself bound by a contract in spite of a mistake or some other defect in its will, or as an outcome of a reasonable interpretation of the contract, which does not conform to the subjective interpretation of that party. Lack of real agreement is also demonstrated in the area of standard form contracts.

32. The conflict between situations that lack true agreement and the concept of contract as based on an agreement is solved by the objective theory. This theory prefers the external indications of the agreement to the undisclosed intention of the parties. Thus, the requirement of the law of contracts is not the meeting of subjective wills, but rather the objective declarations of wills. The objective theory is prominent in various areas of the law of contracts, mainly the area of the formation of the contract (offer and acceptance) and the area of determining its contents (by way of interpretation). The objective theory derives mainly from the need to protect the justified expectations of the contracting parties. It also serves practical needs, such as commercial convenience as well as evidential reasons. Theoretically, agreement is vital for the creation of the contract as well as for its existence. Methodically, agreement is needed for describing and explaining the concept and phenomenon of contract. Practically, real agreement does exist in most contracts.

33. The second element of the definition of contract is enforceability. This element distinguishes contracts from mere agreements. Enforceability indicates the recognition accorded by the general legal system of contracts made by private citizens. This recognition can be direct, by enforcement, or indirect, by awarding damages. By this recognition of contracts, the legislature prescribes the general framework for individuals to express their wishes.

34. The contract is therefore an expression of the parties' will, which is accorded legal recognition. Through the contracts that they make, the contracting parties implement their will and prescribe the law that will apply to their affairs. When individuals operate within the framework of the law, and their mutual wills are channelled into accepted patterns, their agreement will be recognized, and their contract will be enforced. By recognizing the effect and obligatory power of contracts, the sovereign transfers part of its legislating power to the parties. In this manner individuals are accorded the power to create legal-contractual relations.

§2. Historical Background of the Law of Contracts

35. Israeli contract law began its process of development in the middle of the nineteenth century, during the period when Israel (then known as 'Palestine') formed part of the Ottoman Empire. From that era onward, until the establishment of the independent State of Israel in 1948, Israeli contract law was in a constant process of development and transition; from a continentally oriented Ottoman code, through the English judge-made law, to the new original Israeli legislation, based on various sources of law.

36. Until 1921, Palestine formed part of the Ottoman Empire. Two main laws regulated contract law during that period: the Mejelle and the Ottoman code of civil procedure. The books of the Mejelle, the Ottoman Code of Civil Law, regulated important contractual transactions, such as sale and lease. The Mejelle was created in the spirit and principles of the French Code Napoleon, combined with traditional principles, borrowed from Islamic law. The Ottoman Code of Civil Procedure also included important contractual provisions, such as section 64, which established the principle of freedom of contract. By virtue of this section, validity was conferred upon all contracts except for those contrary to statutory law, morality and public order. The power of the parties to contract out of the provisions of the Mejelle was thus accorded recognition.

37. The face of the law of Palestine changed in 1921, after the succession of the Ottoman Empire in the Middle East by the British Empire. The new legal system, introduced by the British, was defined by Article 46 of the Palestine Order in Council 1922. Article 46 provided for the continued application of the Ottoman law then in force in Palestine. In addition, the courts were given residuary powers, regarding the filling of *lacunae*, by the absorption of English common law and equity. The directive of Article 46, coupled with the education and tendencies of the Mandatory judges, led to a situation in which the English component of contract law became the principal and more significant one. It may be said that the bulk of contract law, applied until the establishment of the State of Israel in 1948, was in practice similar, indeed almost identical, to English contract law.

38. The establishment of the independent State of Israel, in 1948, did not cause radical changes in contract law. In accordance with section 11 of the Law and Administration Ordinance 1948, Israeli law assumed the Mandatory Law, which had applied prior to the state's independence. This Mandatory Law comprised of two main components: Ottoman law and English law. English law continued to serve as a principal source for the filling of *lacunae*, and almost all contract law was drawn from that system. At the same time, Israeli judiciary displayed a tendency towards independent policy-making. As a result, the application of English law was restrained, particularly in those areas in which the English rule did not seem desirable, such as in the question of whether consideration should be deemed an indispensable element for the creation of a contract. There were also areas in which the Israeli courts adopted an independent attitude which was different from that of English law, as was the case with regard to the formulation of the remedy of specific performance.

39. The new era in Israeli contract law began in the early 1960s. Since then there has been a wave of original legislation, both in the area of the civil law in general, and in the field of contract law in particular. In the field of contract law there are three general laws as well as a number of special laws pertaining to specific contracts. The three general laws are: the General Contracts Law, 1973; the Remedies Law, 1970, and the Standard Contracts Law, 1982. The special laws are: the Capacity and Guardianship Law, 1962, the Agency Law, 1965, the Sale Law, 1968, the Gift Law, 1967, the Transfer of Obligations Law, 1969, the Hire and Loan Law, 1971, the Contracts for Services Law, 1974 and the Insurance Contract Law, 1981.

40. Simultaneously with the growth of this legislation, the link with the past has been gradually severed. Israeli law was emancipated from English law by law provisions of autarky in specific laws, by the abrogation of the remnants of the Mejelle, and finally, by the Foundations of Law Act 1980, in which the formal link to English law was severed.

§3. Classification of Contracts

41. Israeli General Contracts Law does not distinguish between different types of contracts.[5] Yet, in 2019, two Judges of the Supreme Court, in a decision concerning interpretation of contracts, attempted to classify contracts into certain categories.[6]

5. However, Israeli contract law does recognize specific contracts, like sale of goods. For further discussion regarding these specific contracts, *see* Part II, *infra.*
6. *Bibi Roads & Development Ltd. v. Israel Railways Ltd* (2019). This judgment revisited the discussion regarding contract interpretation. For further discussion, *see* paras 283–289.

42. One of the judges in that case distinguished between relational and contingent contracts, while the other judge classified contracts according to their contracting parties. Although both judges reached the same conclusion, namely that the contract between the Israel Railway Co. and the development company should be interpreted narrowly and literally, their paths to that conclusion were different. While one judge based his conclusion on the contract being a 'completely contingent'contract, the other judge viewed the contract as a commercial contract, where all parties are sophisticated business entities.

§4. Contract and Torts

43. Israeli tort law is embodied in the Civil Wrongs Ordinance (new version). This Ordinance came into force in 1947, during the period of the British mandate. Accordingly, the ordinance compiled and codified English common law on torts, as it existed at that time in England. Since the establishment of the State of Israel, in 1948, Israeli tort law began to develop independently, while being guided by the innovations taking place within English and American common law. The Israeli legislature also enriched Israeli Tort Law by adding new enactments dealing with special problems of tort law, such as the Prevention of Nuisance Law 1961, the Defamation Law 1965, and the Liability for Defective Products Law 1980.

44. Theoretically, contract law and tort law are similar and interrelated areas of law. Both contract law and tort law form part of the larger area of law, called the 'law of obligations'. This concept derived from Roman law, where contract and tort both create an *obligation*. Both contract law and tort law recognize the existence of a primary obligation and a secondary obligation. The primary obligation is the duty of a person, subject to the obligation, to act in some defined manner, in order to fulfil his duties towards the other party. In contract law, the primary obligation is the duty to perform the contract; in tort law, the primary obligation is the duty to avoid certain forms of tortious behaviour, defined by law, and to act with due care towards the other person. Once the primary obligation is breached, the secondary obligation arises – to compensate and indemnify the injured party, and to pay for the damage that had occurred, following the breach of the primary duty.

45. The main theoretical difference between contract law and tort law lies in the source and contents of the primary obligation. In contract law the primary obligation is based on the agreement made between the parties. In tort law the primary obligation is derived from the requirements of law, to act in due care and according to the standards of behaviour prescribed by law.

46. In the past, the difference between the sources of the primary obligation was crucial. In contract law, the number and variety of the primary duties was, and still is, endless, and depends only on the creative imagination of the contracting parties and the rapidly changing demands of commercial life. At the same time, in tort law, the primary obligations and their contents were numbered and well-defined civil wrongs, including a closed list of prohibited modes of behaviour, defined by law.

Today, after the establishment of the general negligence rule as formulated in the famous English case of *Donoghue v. Stevenson*,[7] the primary obligations in tort law are a large variety of vaguely defined forms of behaviour. The *Donoghue* case had opened the list of tortious acts and widened the variety of primary obligations.

47. In the area of the secondary obligation, the resemblance is more obvious. The rule governing the calculation of compensation was first introduced into the common law in the case of *Hadley v. Baxendale*.[8] According to the rules established in this case, the party in breach is responsible for the damage that a reasonable man can foresee or expect to occur, following the breach of the primary obligation.

48. In spite of the theoretical resemblance, the specific practical arrangements in contract law and tort law are usually quite different. Sometimes, the breach of a contractual obligation may be followed by a breach of a tortious obligation, and vice versa; e.g., when the existence of contractual relations may also be a cause for a special duty of care, as defined by the negligence rule. Common examples of these kinds of situations are the various forms of contracts for the performance of services, such as the contract between a doctor and a patient. The death of the patient as a result of the doctor's negligent medical treatment is obviously a tortious act, but it is also a breach of the doctor's contractual duty. In this case, the injured person has two causes of action: the tortious act and the breach of contract. The injured person can either choose one cause of action, or sue in both contract and tort (though he will not be granted double compensation for the same act).

49. The parties to the contract can predetermine their tortious liability by exemption clauses – a common phenomenon in today's contracts. Israeli contract law has developed special doctrines to handle this phenomenon. The first is the doctrine of public policy as defined in section 30 of the Contracts General Law, dealing primarily with exemption clauses for physical injuries. The second doctrine is embodied in the Standard Contracts Law, 1982, and concerns different kinds of exemption clauses in standard contracts.

§5. Contract and Quasi-contract

50. The doctrine of quasi-contracts is enacted in the Israeli legal system in the Unjust Enrichment Law, 1979.[9]

51. The title of the Law reflects an Israeli original attempt within the doctrine of quasi-contracts. Initially the Israeli legislature had rejected suggestions to various

7. *Donoghue v. Stevenson* (1932) AC 562.
8. *Hadley v. Baxendale* (1854) 156 ER 145.
9. For further discussion, *see* paras 759–767.

possible titles for the doctrine of quasi-contract, and adopted the title 'unjust enrichment' – which first appeared in the Bible.[10] However, the American doctrine of restitution, as defined in the Restatement, influences the Israeli doctrine of unjust enrichment.

52. The Unjust Enrichment Law does not encompass a comprehensive doctrine of unjust enrichment. Several important issues, such as tracing, payment made in error, restitution following rescission of a contract or restitution following breach of contract, are not regulated in this Law. These issues are discussed in other laws, such as the Agency Law, 1965, the Trust Law, 1979 and mainly the General Contracts Law, 1973 and the Remedies Law, 1970.[11]

53. Section 1 of the Unjust Enrichment Law provides as follows:

> (a) Where a person obtains any property, service or other benefit from another person without legal cause (the two persons hereinafter respectively referred to as 'the beneficiary' and 'the benefactor'), the beneficiary shall make restitution to the benefactor, and if restitution in kind is impossible or unreasonable shall pay him the value of the benefit.
> (b) It shall be immaterial whether the benefit was obtained through an act of the beneficiary or an act of the benefactor or in any other way.

54. The obligation of restitution, as stipulated in section 1 of the Law, arises upon the fulfilment of three conditions: enrichment, not in accordance with a legal right and on account of the benefactor. In determining the obligation of restitution, considerations of justice and fairness will be applied to the issue of the defendant's enrichment alone.

55. The General Contracts Law and the Unjust Enrichment Law are both part of the law of obligations. However, these two areas are based on entirely different principles. The contractual obligation is a voluntary one, and the damages awarded upon breach of the contract are intended to compensate for losses suffered following the breach. The unjust enrichment obligation is an obligation enforced by law, and intended to prevent the enrichment of the defendant.

56. The intertwined connection between contract law and unjust enrichment law demands special precaution when dealing with causes of action pursuant to the Unjust Enrichment Law and the Remedies Law. As a matter of principle, the cause of action under the Unjust Enrichment Law is a residuary cause. Occasionally, however, the injured party may claim for unjust enrichment although a valid contract exists between the parties, if that contract was breached albeit not rescinded. In such circumstances, the injured party may choose between the causes of action, or claim

---

10. Jeremiah 17.11.
11. For further discussion of restitution following rescission, *see* paras 264–267; 517–520.

on the basis of the two causes, as long as there is no contradiction between them.[12] Thus, the injured party cannot demand restitution and enforcement at the same time, nor be compensated twice for his damage.

§6. Contract and the Law of Property

57. The Israeli law of property includes the Land Law, 1969, the Chattels Law, 1971, the Inheritance Law, 1965 and the Trust Law, 1979.

58. The sources of this legislation are various. The Israeli law of property was legislated following a long period of research into various legal systems; the result is a modern and functional law in tune with the rapidly changing demands of modern commercial life. The characteristics of this legislation mainly originate from continental law, especially French and German-law, with the exception of trust law, which followed the common law doctrine. However, the legal reasoning and the principles of interpretation and jurisprudence are still influenced by the common law.

59. The distinction between the law of property and the law of obligation, including the law of contract, follows the classic distinction between *ius in rem* and *ius in personam*. The first kind of rights is typical of property law, while the rights of the second kind are typical of contract law.

60. Another distinction between the law of obligation and the law of property is the possibility to create different rights. In contract law the principle of freedom of contract requires that parties remain free to form their own contract. However, this is impossible in the law of property. According to Israeli law, property rights are included in a closed list, and no new rights can be added to it by the parties.

§7. Contract and Trust

61. The Israeli trusts doctrine is embodied in the Trust Law, 1979. This law replaced the Ottoman Law of trusts, based on the Muslim Law, and the mandatory Charitable Trusts Ordinance 1922. The Joint Investments in Trust Law, 1961, forms part of the banking laws and deals with investments in trust funds. The Israeli doctrine of trusts is based mainly on Common Law, and its concepts are unfamiliar to Continental Law.

62. A trust, according to section 1 of the Trust Law, is a relationship to property by virtue of which a trustee is bound to hold the same interest, or to act, in respect thereof, in the interest of a beneficiary or for some other purpose. This formula is much wider than the common law doctrine of trust. It includes various situations in

12. *Adras Construction Co. Ltd. v. Harlow & Jones G.M.B.H.* (1988) 42(1) PD 221. This decision is further discussed at 768–770.

which one person is dealing with another person's property for the benefit of the latter, be it a manager, an employee or an agent. There is no legal limitation in the law as to who may be a fiduciary, and the trustee does not obtain ownership in the trust assets, as demanded by the common law doctrine. The only limit on the fiduciary's rights is his duty to act for the benefit of the beneficiary. The fiduciary is granted powers and competence to act according to his discretion and his good judgment in the trust's assets, even if he does not have a property right in them.

63. The beneficiary in Israeli law has an obligatory right against the fiduciary, but he does not have a property right in the trust's assets.

64. A trust can be created by a contract. In this case, the duties of the fiduciary to possess or to act in respect of the trust's assets are provided for by the contract. The contract will also govern the beneficiary's rights or the rights of his parties.

65. The contract creating a trust is regulated by contract law and trust law. The basic principle is that of the freedom of contract, which enables the parties to create their own trust. The law of trusts adds several duties to contract law which are enforceable against the fiduciary; part of these duties are enforced only where there is no other arrangement between the parties (*ius dispositivum*), while others are enforced in spite of the existence of a contradicting arrangement (*ius cogens*).

§8. Freedom of Contract and Good Faith

66. Two main principles govern Israeli contract law: freedom of contract and good faith. The principle of freedom of contract was recognized as one of the basic principles underlying Israel's social and legal system. Although the Basic Law: Human Dignity and Liberty does not expressly mention this principle, and therefore does not explicitly protect this freedom, freedom of contract is considered – in court decisions as well as in academic writings – a leading principle of Israeli contract law. In a leading Supreme Court decision, interpretation of the term 'property' in Basic Law: Human Dignity and Liberty was interpreted as including and protecting contractual rights.[13]

67. Nevertheless, the principle of freedom of contract is not an absolute one. Freedom of contract is balanced and restrained while applying various other principles.

68. One such constraint on the principle of freedom of contract is embodied in the Standard Contracts Law. Under the Standard Contracts Law, the tribunal and the court have the authority to invalidate a condition in a standard contract if it is deemed unduly disadvantageous to customers.[14]

---

13. *Bank Hamizrachi v. Migdal* (1995) 49(4) PD 221.
14. For further discussion, *see* paras 322–345.

69. Other constraints come in the form of *ius cogens* arrangements, namely specific statutory provisions that apply despite any contrary agreement of the parties. These include, *inter alia*, provisions that require the contract to be made according to a certain form, provisions that determine the content of the contract and provisions that impose certain duties on the contractual parties.

70. The court may also intervene in the content of a contract while exercising its power under the Remedies Law. Thus, the court is permitted to decrease the amount of liquidated damages if the amount agreed upon by the parties is deemed unreasonable. The court is also authorized to deny issuing an order of specific performance if doing so is presumed unjust under the circumstances.[15]

71. Perhaps the most prominent constraint on the principle of freedom of contract lies in the provisions of the General Contracts Law that require the parties to act in accordance with a certain moral behavioural standard. These statutory provisions include sections 12 and 39 of the General Contracts Law, which require good faith in negotiations and in the performance of the contract. Another statutory provision is embodied in section 30 of the General Contracts Law which states that illegal contracts as well as contracts contrary to public policy are void. The abovementioned provisions expand judicial power to intervene in contracts, and therefore constitute an effective mechanism for judicial control over contractual relationships.

72. The principle of good faith is also of utmost importance in Israeli contract law. This principle is embodied in sections 12 and 39 of the General Contracts Law, the first section referring to the stage of pre-contractual negotiations, the second to the stage of fulfilling the contract. Through section 61(b) of the same Law, which applies the provisions of the Law to legal acts other than contracts and to obligations not rising out of a contract, the principle of good faith has been applied to many other areas of civil as well as public law.[16]

73. Section 39 of the General Contracts Law requires that contractual rights shall be used and obligations shall be performed in customary manner and in good faith. This section imports parameters of an essentially ethical nature into the legal framework. Nevertheless, once this ethical principle has gained legal validity, it must be applied in accordance with realistic requirements of human conduct. And, indeed, in applying the principle of good faith, some equilibrium was found between its ethical source and societal, commercial needs. The principle of good faith rejects individualism and egotism, but does not necessitate complete altruism. The general requirement to act in customary manner and in good faith is looked upon as a balanced requirement of solidarity and cooperation for the purpose of fulfilling the goals of the contract.

---

15. For further discussion, *see* paras 478–479.
16. For further discussion regarding the duty to act in good faith in pre-contractual negotiations, *see* paras 143–171.

74. The test established in section 39 is an objective one, in the sense that it is concerned with reasonable conduct that is to be expected from a party to a contract, according to general criteria. Certain subjective elements, however – such as the nature of the venture and some characteristics of the parties – are inevitably included as well.

75. The concept of good faith cannot be independently defined or induced to rigid rules – it acquires substance from the particular events that take place and to which it is applied. The difficulty of defining the good faith principle also results from the fact that it is not intended to dictate certain modes of approved behaviour, but rather to negate them.

76. The methodically correct way to describe and understand the concept of good faith is in concrete casuistic terms. This indeed has been the test established by the Israeli Supreme Court: rather than a system of rigid rules, the Court has preferred a gradual and careful case-by-case development, eventually giving rise to guidelines and rules for the application of the principle of good faith. Nevertheless, in spite of the absence of a *numerus clausus* of situations that section 39 applies to, restraints have been placed on the application of this principle – particularly so as not to unnecessarily injure the dynamics of commerce and free enterprise, the principle of freedom of contract and the expectations of the parties.

77. The central question in any application of section 39 will be whether the means employed by the parties conform to the requirement of good faith. The answer differs from one case to another according to the particular circumstances of each case. Certain means may be considered to lack good faith in one given contractual situation, while conforming to the requirement of good faith in another. Thus, lack of diligence in performing a contract, non-disclosure of material information or any other act or omission that are hostile to the spirit of the transaction and its purpose, will be considered as a breach of the duty to perform the contract in good faith, a duty embodied in section 39.

78. Section 39 applies the principle of good faith to the fulfilment of contractual obligations in addition to the exercise of contractual rights. However, only certain circumstances may indicate that a party, acting within his rights, has violated the duty of good faith. The use of tricks, sophistry or the attempt to cause losses to the other party can indicate that contractual rights were used in bad faith.

79. The principle of good faith applies not only to the contracting parties but also guides the court. When interpreting a contract, the court must interpret it in good faith, namely with regard to the parties' genuine intent. Similarly, the act of supplementation must also be carried out according to the principle of good faith.

When the parties' intent is characterized as ambiguous, or when the contract contains a *lacuna* in need of supplementation, the court may interpret the contract – or in some cases, fill in the gap – utilizing the principle of good faith.[17]

80. The principle of good faith applies in other contexts as well. In the past, the court explored the possibility of adjusting the contractual price during periods of high inflation, relying on the principle of good faith.

81. In exceptional circumstances, the principle of good faith is utilized to overcome the formal requirement for written documentation that applies to contracts for the sale of land.[18]

82. A contracting party that does not fulfil contractual obligations in good faith or does not use contractual rights in good faith is in breach of the contract. Such a breach entitles the other party to remedies awarded upon breach of contract, namely enforcement, damages and rescission. The results of non-compliance with the good faith principle are not limited to the traditional remedies.[19] The court may resort to the principle of good faith in determining that one of the contracting parties was not free to exercise his right of rescission. In addition, the court can decide that a party that does not uphold his contractual obligations is precluded, by virtue of the principle of good faith, from demanding the other party to uphold his contractual obligations.

§9. Style of Drafting

83. Israeli contract law is inspired by and modelled after European codes. The formulation of the statutes governing contracts avoids details and is abstract and general, simple and concise in style. It reflects a way of thinking based on general principles, a definite departure from Anglo-Saxon method. In accordance with the change of the substantive law, Israeli modern contracts are now shorter and simpler than they used to be under the regime of English Common Law. The Israeli drafter, like its European counterpart, works within a framework provided by the statutory law – a framework of general and particular rules appropriate for any specific and given kind of contract.

§10. Sources of the Law of Contracts

I. General

84. Contract law in Israel is embodied in various statutes. These statutes are formulated and enacted as separate laws. The sources of the legislation in the field of

17. For further discussion, *see* para. 312.
18. For further discussion, *see* para. 124.
19. Cf. Barak J. in *Transportation Services in Beer Sheba v. Labour Tribunal* (1980) 35(1) PD 828, 834.

contracts are many and varied, based on long research into various legal systems. Amongst them are the following sources of inspiration and guidance.

II. International Treaties

85. Draft laws arose as a result of the activity of international committees for the unification of private law. The Sale Law, 1968, and, in its wake the Hire and Loan Law, 1971, were influenced by the Uniform Law for the International Sale of Goods. Also drawn from this Law are the provisions of the first chapter of the General Contracts Law, dealing with offer and acceptance.[20]

III. Continental Codes

86. Continental Codes influenced the law of contract in legislative technique as well as in substantive provisions. The legislative technique of the General Contracts Law is essentially similar to the technique employed in the French Code Civile, which prefers broad provisions, instead of the more detailed technique of the German B.G.B. However, the principle of good faith, which was derived from section 242 of the B.G.B., is prominent on the substantive side.[21]

IV. English Law

87. The influence of English law, which in the past reigned supreme in contract law, is particularly noticeable among the sources of Israeli contract law. Thus, English common law influenced directly specific laws (Transfer of Obligations, Agency, Trusts), as well as some provisions of the General Contracts Law (Chapter 6: Several Debtors and Creditors), and of the Remedies Law (section 10 dealing with damages and adopting the classical foreseeability test for damages in the common law; section 17 dealing with anticipatory breach).[22]

V. Jewish Law

88. The influence of Jewish law on the new legislation is somewhat less prominent than its proponents had hoped. Such influence is noticeable mainly in the wording of some provisions of the General Contracts Law, like the expression 'resolve' in section 2. The influence of Jewish law can also be seen in places where the substantive provisions are similar to the provisions of foreign codes. Thus, for example, the provisions of Chapter 4 of the General Contracts Law, which are apparently

20. For further discussion, *see* paras 91–108.
21. For further discussion, *see* paras 72 et seq.
22. For further discussion, *see* paras 384–395 (transfer of obligations); 562–574 (agency); 61–65 (trust); 525–532 (foreseeability test); 460–464 (anticipatory breach).

taken from the B.G.B., are, at the same time, similar to the approach of ancient Jewish law. A certain degree of influence of Jewish law is also reflected in the Bailees Law, and possibly in section 31 of the General Contracts Law, dealing with the result of an illegal contract.[23]

VI. Israeli Case Law

89. Certain innovations of the General Contracts Law, enacted twenty-five years after the independence of the State of Israel, are derived from earlier case law. Thus, for example, in section 14(d) of the General Contracts Law, the distinction between mistake of fact and mistake of law was abolished, following decisions in which this distinction had been criticized.[24] The regulation concerning a contract to award a mark, title or prize, prescribed in section 33 of the General Contracts Law, also addresses problems which had arisen in the case law that preceded the enactment of the General Contracts Law.[25]

VII. Israeli Statutory Law

90. Section 18 of the General Contracts Law, dealing with extortion, contains elements similar to those of the offence prescribed in section 431 of the Penal Law, 1977.[26]

23. For further discussion, *see* para. 93 (s. 2 of the General Contracts Law); paras 373–383 (Ch. 4 of the General Contracts Law); paras 268–277 (s. 31 of the General Contracts Law).
24. *Japhet v. Eastwood* (1969) 23(1) PD 604, 613; *Hai v. Cohen* (1971) 25(2) PD 339.
25. For further discussion, *see* paras 618–624.
26. For further discussion, *see* paras 226–237.

Part I. General Principles of the Law of Contract

Chapter 1. Formation

§1. Agreement and 'Quid Pro Quo' (Reciprocity)

I. Offer and Acceptance

91. Section 1 of the General Contracts Law provides as follows:

> A contract is made by way of offer and acceptance...

92. Offer and acceptance are declarations of the parties' will. These declarations must manifest the parties' consent to make a contract with each other. The consent of the parties is determined by an objective test: when determining whether a party has consented, the court will evaluate the external appearance of the party's intentions as manifested by its actions. According to the objective theory, the parties' actions and words together with the circumstances of the case, judged by a standard of reasonableness, must manifest an intention to enter the contract, while the unexpressed state of mind of the parties is irrelevant.

93. A second requirement that must be met in order for a contract to be recognized – consent being the first – is that of definiteness. This requirement stems from section 2 of the General Contracts Law, stating that one person's proposal for another person constitutes an offer if it is 'sufficiently definite to enable the contract to be concluded by acceptance of the offer'. A proposal that is precise and detailed, in a way that it can be accepted without need for further negotiation, will be considered sufficiently definite. The same will hold for a proposal that is not as detailed and precise, but can be supplemented by the court. Yet, a minimum of definiteness is always necessary, that minimum being the general framework of the transaction and its basic vital elements.

94. The Israeli Supreme Court has demonstrated a flexible approach in determining which details are considered basic and vital to the contract.[27] There is no list

27. *Kadari v. The Order of the Sisters of St. Charles* (1976) 30 (i) *P.D.* 800.

of core elements which, in their absence, the contract is deemed indefinite. Rather, the Supreme Court established a test that considers the parties' intent and the particular circumstances of each case.

95. A contract is made when notice of acceptance from the offeree has been delivered to the offeror (section 5 of the General contracts Law). According to section 60(b) of the Law, a notice 'shall be taken to have been served when it reached the addressee or his address'. Namely, in order for a contract to be concluded, the notice of acceptance must reach the offeror or his address. The notice must attest to the offeree's resolve to enter into the contract with the offeror in accordance with his offer.

96. For purposes of venue and choice of law, a contract is deemed to be made where the notice of acceptance is delivered.

97. Section 6(a) of the Law provides that:

> Acceptance may be by an act in implementation of the contract or by some other conduct if these modes of acceptance are implied in the offer; and for the purposes of sections 3(a) and 4(2), conduct as aforesaid is treated as notification of acceptance

98. Conduct is treated as acceptance whenever such conduct is implied in the offer and attests to the party's consent. Even more so, conduct can be treated as notification of acceptance for deciding whether the offer was withdrawn and whether the time of acceptance has elapsed.

99. Section 6(b) provides:

> A declaration by an offeror that the absence of any response on the part of the offeree shall be regarded as acceptance is of no effect.

100. Silence by itself cannot be interpreted as acceptance, unless there are external circumstances indicating the offeree's consent.

101. The General Contracts Law does not explicitly include the distinction between an offer and an invitation to treat (or to deal), but this distinction conforms to the analysis of the Law. A proposal that does not manifest the offeror's consent to make a contract or that is not sufficiently definite to enable a contract to be concluded by its acceptance, can be considered as an invitation to treat.

102. The distinction between an invitation to treat and an offer is to be applied in situations of proposals made to the public, in order to determine whether such proposals are offers that can be accepted by individuals or mere invitations to treat. Typical cases are advertisement, catalogue-sales and displays of goods in shop windows, supermarkets, vending machines, prizes, tenders and auctions.

103. Section 3 of the Law deals with withdrawal of an offer. Section 3(a) provides:

> The offeror may withdraw the offer by notice to the offeree, provided that the notice of withdrawal is delivered to the offeree before he has given notice of acceptance.

104. Section 3(a) creates a peculiar intermediate hybrid legal situation. In this situation a contract has not yet been concluded and therefore is not binding the parties to it, but the offeror may not withdraw his offer.

105. Section 3(b) provides:

> Where the offeror has declared that the offer is irrevocable or has set a time for its acceptance, he may not withdraw it after it has been delivered to the offeree.

106. This section recognizes the concept of an irrevocable offer. According to this subsection, an offer can be deemed irrevocable in two types of circumstances: where the offeror has declared that the offer is irrevocable or where the offeror has set a time for the offer's acceptance. An irrevocable offer cannot be withdrawn after it has been delivered to the offeree.

107. An offer lapses when the offeree has rejected it or the time for its acceptance has elapsed. In the absence of a specific period, the offer must be accepted within reasonable time. Late acceptance or acceptance with variation is equivalent to a new offer, this time by the offeree (sections 8(a) and 9 of the Law).

108. The theoretical model set out in section 1 of the General Contracts Law, namely that of a contract made by way of offer and acceptance, represents the classical model of creating a contract. It is important to note that this model is merely a methodological form of analysis that helps determine whether a contract has been formed. Yet, a contract can be formed through different means so long as it reflects the agreement of both parties. Accordingly, a more flexible model provides that the formation of a contract does not begin – chronologically or substantially – with a consolidated offer, but rather through a process of pre-contractual negotiations, during which the requirements for mutual consent and definiteness are met.

II. Intention to Create Legal Relations

109. Israeli law requires an intention to create legal relations as a substantive element for an effective contract. This requirement is especially important in a legal system – like the Israeli system – where there is no additional requirement of consideration or cause.

110. The requirement of an intention to create legal (contractual) relations stems from the general concept of contract under Israeli law. According to this concept, a contract is the result of the mutual will of the parties, and it will not come into existence without such will.

111. The parties' will must therefore be accompanied by an intention to create legal-contractual relations. An agreement will effectively bind the parties only providing they had intended for it to do so. The existence of such mutual intention is determined according to an objective test.

III. Consideration

112. During the period prior to the enactment of the General Contracts Law in 1973, the bulk of contract law in Israel relied on English law.[28] Yet, Israeli judges had not surrendered to the Common Law doctrine of consideration. This doctrine was rejected more than once, although it never became clear whether, before 1973, an 'Israeli contract' could be concluded without consideration.

113. Since the enactment of the General Contracts Law, it is evident that Israeli law does not require consideration as an element of a binding contract. This Law dispensed with the requirement of consideration, by referring only to offer and acceptance as elements essential to the making of contracts.

IV. Modifications of the Contract

114. The Common Law rule of consideration was extended to the area of discharge or modification of contracts. As Israeli law does not include the requirement of consideration, modification of a contract under Israeli law requires only an agreement.

§2. Formal and Evidential Requirements

I. Formal Requirements

115. The general rule regarding form of contracts under Israeli law is freedom of form. Section 23 of the General Contracts Law provides:

> A contract may be made orally, in writing or in some other form … .

116. This rule reflects the principle of freedom of contract. The will of the contracting parties governs not only the contents but also the form of the contract. The

28. Discussed above at para. 87.

rule of freedom of form expresses the spirit of modern contract law, which is a spirit of fairness, good faith and lack of formality.

117. The significance of the freedom of form is that the contract may be concluded in any form, but not that it may be made without any form. Some form must exist.

118. A contract 'orally' made is the outcome of an oral offer and an oral acceptance. Even in complicated, serious and expensive matters, a contract does not have to be in writing, as long as the requirements of the law – mainly agreement and definiteness – are met.[29]

119. A contract 'in writing' is a contract made and expressed in a written and signed document. 'Writing' in this context includes modern means of making contracts, like computers, telex, facsimile, video-screen, emails and text messages.

120. A contract 'in some other form' can be a combination of the above-mentioned means, e.g., a written offer orally accepted, or an oral offer followed by a letter of acceptance. A contract may also be made by conduct. Section 6(a) of the General Contracts Law provides that acceptance may be by an act 'in implementation of the contract or by some other conduct … '.

121. The freedom of form, embodied in the first part of section 23 of the General Contracts Law, is not absolute. Section 23 provides, in its second part, two restrictions to the freedom of form. First, when a particular form is a condition of the contract's validity by virtue of law; second, when a particular form is a condition of the contract's validity by virtue of a former agreement between the parties.

122. The provisions of law that require a contract be made according to a certain form can be divided into two groups. The first group includes provisions of law that pertain to form as a substantive element of the contract (*ad substantiam*). The second group includes provisions of law that require a contract to be made according to a certain form in order to *prove* the existence of an agreement (*ad probationem*). A contract will be deemed void only when it does not meet the substantive requirements of the relevant law.

123. The most important provision of law requiring a certain form is section 8 of the Land Law, 1969. This section requires a written document for a transaction in real estate to take effect. In the past, the Israeli Supreme Court interpreted this section as providing a substantive condition of validity, so that unless a written document is made, no transaction in land is effectuated. Yet, gradually, the Supreme Court mitigated this formal requirement. Thus, it was determined that when non-substantial ambiguities occur in a written contract, the gaps in the written document can be supplemented by the court. In such cases, the document will be considered sufficiently definite and the transaction will take effect. The Supreme Court also held

29. For further discussion, *see* paras 28–34.

that the parties' signature in itself is not essential to the fulfilment of the form requirement. These rulings are consistent with the general tendency of the Supreme Court to interpret provisions of law that require a contract to be made according to a certain form, as an evidentiary requirement rather than as a substantive one.

124. Over the years, the formal requirements of the above-mentioned section 8 of the Land Law were mitigated, culminating with a ruling by the Supreme Court that in special circumstances the principle of good faith supersedes the formal requirement of documentation. According to this ruling, the performance of an oral contract by one party may prevent the other party from claiming its invalidity due to the fact that it was not formulated in writing. The court stated that 'good faith and writing – good faith prevails'.[30] This ruling was not repeated and was even rejected in a couple of decisions. It was later determined that only in exceptional cases and under certain circumstances good faith supersedes the formal requirements for written documentation.

125. Section 5 of the Gift Law, 1968, also requires a written document in order to give effect to an undertaking to make a gift in the future. This section, too, was interpreted in the past as creating a substantive requirement.

126. The requirement for written documentation also exists in section 19 of the Prescription Law 1958, in section 1 of Law of Property Relations between Spouses, 1973, in section 7 of the Collective Agreements Law, 1957, in section 26 of the Shipping Law (Vessels), 1960 and in section 17 of the Trust Law, 1979.

II. Evidential Requirement: Proof

127. The general rules of evidence regarding contracts (*ad probationem*) are still embodied in remnants of the Ottoman period and of the Common Law.

128. Section 80 of the Ottoman Code of Civil Procedure of 1879 provides that written evidence can only be disproved by another piece of written evidence.

129. The parol evidence rule prohibits contracting parties from providing oral evidence in order to contradict a written contract.

130. Today, the formalistic requirement of documentary evidence to contest a claim based on a written agreement is hardly significant in Israeli contract law. Modern doctrines and principles of interpretation, and mainly the *Aprofim* rule,[31] barely leaves room for the above-mentioned section 80 and the parol evidence rule.

30. *Klemer v. Guy* (1996) 50(1) PD 185.
31. For further discussion, *see* paras 283–289.

III. Burden of Proof

131. The general rule regarding burden of proof in civil cases is that the plaintiffs have to prove their case. Thus, if the defendants have not admitted in their pleadings all the facts claimed by the plaintiffs, the plaintiffs must prove their case. Accordingly, in contract cases, the creditors have to show and prove that the debtors have not performed their obligation.

132. Unlike French law, which draws a distinction between 'obligation of means' (*obligation de moyens*) and 'obligation of result' (*obligation de résultat*), Israeli law usually regards the contractual liability as a strict liability (subject to the good faith principle). In other words, every act or omission in contravention of a contract is usually considered a breach of the contract, regardless of the debtor's intention. Consequently, the rule of burden of proof applies to all kinds of contracts. The plaintiff or creditor has to prove all the elements of their cause of action.

§3. Liability and Negotiations

I. Pre-contractual Liability

A. Introduction

133. The subject of pre-contractual liability was of marginal importance in Israeli law until the enactment of the General Contracts Law. Section 12 of this law, entitled 'good faith in negotiations', signalled the development of a new sphere of Israeli law. Gradually, the application of this provision has been broadened, and further norms from various areas of civil law – torts, unjust enrichment, contracts – have also been applied, together determining the criteria of conduct in pre-contractual negotiations. Section 12 of the General Contracts Law will be discussed further.[32] In the following paragraphs, other areas of civil law pertaining to pre-contractual liability shall be discussed.

B. Law of Torts

134. The law of torts is one of the legal sources that imposes obligations on the parties in the context of the pre-contractual process. Among the civil wrongs, comprising a *numerous clausus* in Israeli law, the causes of action that may apply to the pre-contractual stage are primarily those of fraud and negligence.

135. The civil wrongs of fraud is defined in section 56 of the Civil Wrongs Ordinance (New Version). A party that enters into pre-contractual negotiations without

---

32. *See* paras 143 et seq.

intending to form a contract will be liable, under this provision, where during negotiations he or she knowingly misrepresented a fact, intending that it be acted upon by the other party to the negotiations, and causing, as result, pecuniary damage to the other party.

136. The civil wrongs of negligence is defined in sections 35–36 of the Civil Wrongs Ordinance. Under these provisions, every person is subject to a general obligation to take reasonable measures to prevent damage to a person whom he or she ought to have contemplated as likely to be injured. A specific duty was established within the framework of these general provisions, namely the duty not to provide negligent information and to provide accurate information to a person who relies on such information.[33] The cause of action of negligent representation during negotiations was applied in two decisions of the Supreme Court. In one of them, liability in damages was incurred because of a negligent misrepresentation that took place during pre-contractual negotiations.[34] In the other, the Court held that non-disclosure of relevant facts amounted to breach of duty of non-negligent behaviour.[35]

C. *Unjust Enrichment*

137. The laws of unjust enrichment may also apply to the pre-contractual stage. Restitution in accordance with the laws of unjust enrichment will be granted to a party who had begun to perform the contract but no contract was made at the conclusion of the negotiations. Such cases may occur when the other party intentionally caused the negotiations to break off, or when a contract is not concluded for some entirely legitimate reason, such as the absence of a substantive element of the offer.

138. Situations where the laws of unjust enrichment apply to the pre-contractual process are, for example, cases where a potential buyer pays a deposit for property upon the belief that a contract will be made for its sale, or where a contractor begins performing the work that was ordered, although the price had not yet been established. If no contract is made at the end of the negotiations, the party that paid the deposit will be entitled to restitution, and the contractor will be entitled to fees for the work already performed. The right of a professional to collect fees for services rendered during pre-contractual negotiations has been recognized by the Israeli Supreme Court under the laws of unjust enrichment.[36]

33. This duty was first established in *Weinstein v. Kadima* (1954) 8 PD 1317, where Israeli law preceded English law on negligent misrepresentation by a full decade. *See Hedley Byrne v. Heller* (1963) 2 All ER 574.
34. *American Microsystems Inc. v. Elbit* (1985) 39(2) PD 785, 795–798.
35. *Kaplan v. Novogrozky* (1984) 38(3) PD 477.
36. *Grober v. Tel Yossef* (1981) 35(4) PD 45.

D. Law of Contracts

139. The Law of Contracts itself applies to the pre-contractual stage. Even when the negotiations culminate in a contract, the events, declarations and representations that preceded its formation may gain importance. These are relevant in answering the following questions: Was a contract made at all? If so, when was it made? Was there some defect in the will of one of the parties at a critical moment in the making of the contract? What is the precise content of the contract, and what is the true meaning of its provisions? Were collateral obligations created during the pre-contractual negotiations as an outcome of a preliminary agreement?

140. The pre-contractual process ends with the making of the contract (or, sometimes, with the unsuccessful termination of the negotiations without contractual consequences). Thus, the formation of the contract constitutes part of the pre-contractual process. Under Chapter 1 of the General Contracts Law, a contract is formed when notice of acceptance is delivered to the offeror. Prior to this moment, various stages may take place, such as invitation to treat, offer and revocation of an offer. Chapter 1 of the General Contracts Law regulates these stages in the process of the contract's creation, and the provisions of this Chapter may therefore have relevance to the pre-contractual process.

141. The provisions of Chapter 2 of the General Contracts Law, dealing with defects in formation, also apply to the pre-contractual process. These provisions provide the party whose will was defective with a right to rescind the contract and by their nature oblige examination of events that occurred before the contract was made. The determination of the contents of the contract through interpretation of its provisions requires ascertaining the parties' will, as it materialized at the stage of formation. Such ascertainment sometimes involves examination of events and circumstances that took place during the pre-contractual stage.

142. Various provisions in specific laws also draw attention to the pre-contractual process. An example is section 16 of the Sale Law, 1968, that deals with non-conformity resulting from non-disclosure of facts that the seller knew or should have known at the time of making the contract.

II. Pre-contractual Negotiations

A. The Meaning of the Good Faith Requirement

143. Section 12 of the General Contracts Law is the principal norm governing pre-contractual negotiations in Israeli law. This section provides as follows:

i. In negotiating a contract, a person shall act in customary manner and in good faith.
ii. A party who does not act in customary manner and in good faith shall be liable to pay compensation to the other party for the damage caused to him

in consequence of the negotiations or the making of the contract, and the provisions of sections 10, 13 and 14 of the Contracts (Remedies for Breach of Contract) Law, 5731–1970, shall apply *mutatis mutandis*.

144. Section 12 follows the continental theory of *culpa in contrahendo.*[37] This theory creates a pre-contractual duty to negotiate in good faith and – as a result – liability for compensation, even if no contract was reached at the end of the pre-contractual negotiations. Although section 12 was influenced by the theory of *culpa in contrahendo*, it does not constitute an exact copy or a translation of the above-mentioned doctrine, but rather an independent application of the general principle of good faith to the negotiation stage. The criterion stipulated – 'customary manner and good faith' – is identical to that of section 39 of the General Contracts Law, which deals with the contractual stage and requires that contractual rights shall be exercised and obligations shall be performed in customary manner and in good faith.[38]

B. Analytical Areas of Application

1. General

145. The methodical difficulties in describing the principle of good faith[39] prevent an *a priori* definition of the situations to which section 12 will apply and require a retrospective examination of court decisions in which this section has been applied.

146. Nevertheless, we can examine the application of the norm prescribed in section 12 on three analytical levels: chronological, personal and material.

2. The Chronological Level

147. Section 12 applies from the first encounter between the parties until the making of the contract or until the unsuccessful termination of the negotiations. From the moment that the parties enter into negotiations, their conduct must be examined according to the criterion of section 12. Yet, the weight of the good faith requirement grows as the wishes of the parties and the declarations of their wills gradually crystallize. As the parties to the pre-contractual negotiations approach the contractual territory, the intensity of the duty to act in good faith increases.

37. Friedrich Kessler & Edith Fine, *Culpa in Contrahendo, Bargaining in Good Faith and Freedom of Contract: A Comparative Study,* 77 Harv. L. Rev. 401 (1964).
38. For a discussion of the general principle of good faith, embodied in s. 39, discussed above at paras 71–82.
39. Discussed above at paras 75–76.

148. In addition to its application during pre-contractual negotiations, section 12 also applies to the stage of the making the contract. In this stage, which is governed by Chapter 1 of the General Contracts Law, offer and acceptance meet. The term 'towards' the conclusion of the contract in section 12(a), should be read to include the stage of making the contract itself. Section 12 thus applies to the stage of making the contract, even in situations where no pre-contractual negotiations preceded this stage.

149. This application of section 12 is especially important in the area of standard form contracts, which by their nature are not preceded by a pre-contractual process. The main difficulty of standard form contracts lies in the unilateral nature of their terms.[40] A claim may be made against this unilaterality, not only in terms of undue disadvantage, as provided by the Standard Contracts Law, 1982, but also by means of section 12 of the General Contracts Law. The mere inclusion of unilateral terms in a standard form contract can be considered an infringement of the principle of good faith embodied in section 12.

3. The Personal Level

150. According to the broad interpretation of section 12 in the decisions of the Supreme Court, the section applies to every person who participates in the pre-contractual negotiations, whether or not they eventually become parties to the contract and whether or not a contract was, in fact, made at the conclusion of the negotiations.[41] What determines the personal application of section 12 is the mere participation in the pre-contractual negotiations, rather than the status of a future party to the contract. Section 12 thus applies to agents and directors acting in their capacities, in accordance with the laws of agency and the laws of corporations. In practice, all people who participated in negotiations, regardless of whether they actually became a party to the contract, may be liable to pay compensation according to section 12(b).

4. The Material Level

151. Section 12 applies regardless of whether or not a contract was made at the conclusion of the pre-contractual negotiations and regardless of whether additional causes of action exist.

152. The duty to act in good faith arises independently, due to the pre-contractual negotiations, even if these negotiations do not culminate in a contract. The making of the contract at the conclusion of the negotiations is not a condition

40. For further discussion, *see* paras 322–345.
41. *Pnidar v. Castro*, (1983) 37(4) PD 673.

of the application of section 12. Yet, in addition to the doctrine of *culpa in contrahendo*[42] – which covers situations where a contract was not concluded due to the lack of good faith of a party to the pre-contractual negotiations – section 12 applies also when the pre-contractual negotiations, in which one party did not act in good faith, culminate in a contract.

153. Section 12 provides an independent cause of action and can apply even when the pre-contractual negotiations give rise to another cause of action that enables the rescission or avoidance of the contract. This co-existence of causes of action is most apparent in cases where some defect in the formation of the contract exists, such as a unilateral mistake known to the other party, deceit, duress or extortion (sections 14(a), 15, 17 and 18 of the General Contracts Law).[43]

C. *Concrete Areas of Application*

154. As previously described, the methodically correct way to describe and understand the concept of good faith is in concrete casuistic terms.[44] Namely, the question of whether the pre-contractual negotiations were conducted in good faith cannot be answered without recourse to the particular circumstances of each case. Certain measures can be consistent with the principle of good faith in one negotiation, but contradictory to the principle of good faith in a different negotiation.

1. Parallel Negotiations

155. The proposed methodological analysis can be illustrated by asking whether parallel negotiation with others constitutes an infringement of the principle of good faith. In this context it should be established, for example, whether one party to the negotiations led the other party to believe that no parallel negotiations would take place.

2. The Technique of Conducting Negotiations

156. Raising new and unreasonable demands during negotiations, rejecting reasonable offers put forward by the other party, revoking offers previously made – all of these can amount to lack of good faith in negotiations.

42. *See* Friedrich Kessler & Edith Fine, *supra* note 37.
43. For further discussion, *see* paras 188–193 (unilateral mistake known to the other party), 201–214 (deceit), 215–225 (duress) and 226–237 (extortion).
44. Discussed above at paras 75–76.

3. Non-disclosure

157. A common area of application of the duty to act in good faith in negotiations is the area of discovery. Non-disclosure of facts may constitute a breach of section 12 when, under the circumstances of the case, an expectation was created that the person conducting the negotiations would disclose certain facts to the other party. The duty to act in good faith includes the duty to disclose material facts to the other party during negotiations – even such facts as the other party could have discovered on its own – when such discovery is required by the nature of the transaction and the circumstances of the case.

4. Breaking-Off Negotiations

158. The bond that exists between parties to pre-contractual negotiations is looser than the contractual bond. Pre-contractual negotiations are aimed not only at determining the contents of the eventual contract but also at enabling the parties to decide whether they will enter into a contract to begin with. Therefore, parties to the negotiations have, in principle, the right to break off the negotiations. The only restraint upon this right is derived from the principle of good faith. Breaking-off negotiations in good faith means leaving the negotiations because of reasons that result from the nature of the transaction, the development of the negotiations and the relative strengths of the parties. In every case of breaking-off negotiations, the circumstances of the case should be taken into account; particularly the stage that the negotiations had reached and the reason for breaking off the negotiations. As the parties reach the advanced stages of the negotiations and progress towards the contractual realm, more compelling reasoning will be needed to justify the termination of negotiations.

5. Conducting Negotiations Without Contractual Intent

159. Entering into negotiations without any intention to make a contract, conducting negotiations without intending ultimately to conclude them with a contract and making a contract without intending to execute it, or with knowledge that the contract will be breached: all and any of these may also constitute a breach of section 12.

160. The risk that negotiations will prove unproductive is ever-present, and the right to break off the negotiations is certainly recognized in principle. However, the possibility that, from the outset, the other party to the negotiations had no intention to enter the contract, goes beyond reasonable business expectations, and it is such expectations that section 12 seeks to protect. Conducting negotiations without any real intention of ultimately entering into a contract can be the result of various motives. Such motives include the desire to gain time, to neutralize the other party, to prevent competition by the other party or merely to fulfil a regulatory provision. In each case, such misleading conduct may constitute a breach of the good faith requirement.

6. Illegal Demands

161. A difficult question, which has not yet been resolved in Israeli law, is whether the mere raising of an illegal demand during negotiations amounts to lack of good faith. In a case decided by the Supreme Court, it was contended that the seller of an apartment had demanded, as a condition for signing the contract, that part of the price be paid 'under the table' without being reflected in the written contract, for the purpose of avoiding taxes. The buyers refused to accept this new demand, and the bargain was not concluded. All three judges considered the demand to include a false price in the contract as illegal. However, their opinions varied as to whether the mere raising of such a demand is contrary to the requirement of the principle of good faith.[45]

162. The new constitutional reality created by the enactment of two new basic laws – Basic Law: Human Dignity and Liberty and Basic Law: Freedom of Occupation – has increased the weight of the principle of good faith in Israel's contract law. According to a modern approach, advocated by Chief Justice Barak, public law values (such as equality) can be applied in private law via the conduit of section 12 and the 'valve concept' of good faith.[46]

163. The legislation of the Prohibition of Discrimination in Products, Services and Entry into Places of Entertainment and Public Places Law, 2000, follows this modern approach. The law prohibits anyone who supplies goods or a public service or who operates a public place from discriminating against potential clients.[47] This Law introduces the principle of equality into the pre-contractual process.

D. Remedies

164. Section 12(b) provides for the common remedy that may be claimed upon a breach of the duty to act in customary manner and in good faith during negotiations, namely:

> compensation to the other party for the damage caused to him in consequence of the negotiations or the making of the contract … .

---

45. *Sonnenstein v. Gabsso* (1988) 42(2) PD 278.
46. Discussed above at paras 24–25.
47. Discussed above at para. 26.

165. The word 'or' in section 12(b) indicates that compensation for breach of the duty to act in good faith during the pre-contractual negotiations may be claimed whether negotiations amount to a final binding contract or not.

166. Compensation according to section 12(b) are awarded 'for the damage caused ... ' to the injured party. Section 12(b) has been interpreted as protecting the reliance interest of the injured party.[48] The reliance interest is protected by negative damages, the aim of which is *restitutio in integrum*, namely placing the injured party back in the same position that he or she occupied on the eve of the negotiations.

167. A remedy that protects the reliance interest typically compensates for reasonable expenses incurred by the injured party as a result of his or her reliance on the completion of the proposed transaction. Reliance damages include the following: expenses incurred by the injured party towards the conclusion of the contract like payment of brokerage fees; tender fees; attorney's fees and other expenses involved; expenses made in order to ensure the fulfilment of an obligation, such as down payments or other payments paid to the seller; expenses made in preparation for the transaction, like the purchase of equipment necessary for the execution of the contract. Expenses and investments made with the aim of increasing the expected profit from the contract are also included in the remedy of section 12(b). Protecting the reliance interest within section 12(b) may also include pecuniary damages for lost alternative opportunities.

168. Damages pursuant to section 12(b) can be awarded together with rescission of the contract due to a defect in its formation.[49]

169. In a long series of Supreme Court decisions, negative damages have constituted the sole remedy for breach of section 12(a). However, Former Chief Justice Barak expressed the view that there may be exceptions where it will be possible to claim positive damages within the framework of section 12(b). These are cases in which the pre-contractual negotiations reached a very advanced stage of near-closure, whereby the parties were familiar with the terms of the contract and it was only the lack of good faith that prevented the conclusion of the contract at the very last moment.[50]

170. Chief Justice Barak's opinion is open to criticism, based on the language of section 12, as well as on its *ratio legis*. The remedies for breach of section 12(a) are limited to those mentioned in section 12(b). Section 12 ought to be read as a whole, with each subsection relating to the other. The only remedies accorded for breach of section 12(a) are those mentioned in section 12(b), namely, pecuniary damages that protect the reliance interest of the injured party. The application of further remedies would make section 12(b) superfluous.

---

48. The origin of this distinction lies in the landmark article: Lon L. Fuller & William R. Jr. Perdue, *The Reliance Interest in Contract Damages*, 46 Yale L. J. 52 (1936/7).
49. For further discussion of defects in formation, *see* paras 172 et seq.
50. *Kal Binyan v. E.R.M.* (2002) 56(3) PD 289.

171. Although the opinion of Chief Justice Barak was mentioned a few times in court decisions, it was rarely applied. The Supreme Court clarified that the remedy for the breach of section 12(a) is reliance damages, namely negative pecuniary damages.

Chapter 2. Conditions of Substantive Validity

§1. Capacity of the Parties

172. Israeli law distinguishes between two kinds of capacity: capacity in respect of rights and obligations and capacity in respect of legal acts. This distinction is derived from the German and Suisse Codes.

173. The first kind of capacity, capacity in respect of rights and obligations, is addressed within section 1 of the Capacity and Guardianship Law, 1962. According to this section every person is capable of having rights and obligations from the moment of his birth until the time of his death. This kind of capacity is identical to the concept of the juridical person.

174. The second kind of capacity, capacity in respect of legal acts, is also provided for in the Capacity and Guardianship Law, 1962. This capacity, namely, capacity to perform legal acts, is restricted by means of two exceptions: minority and a court's declaration of a person as being legally incompetent.

175. Contracts of minors or persons who have been declared incompetent require the consent of their representatives. Consent may be given in advance or after the formation of a contract and may refer to a particular contract or a class of contracts. The representative may withdraw his consent as long as the contract has not been performed.

176. Contracts made by minors or persons who have been declared legally incompetent may be avoided. This avoidance can be performed by the minor's or the incompetent person's representative, or, if they have no representative, by the Attorney General, within a month after the contract has come to their knowledge. If the contract has not come to the knowledge of the representative or the Attorney General, it can be avoided by the minor, within a month from attaining full age, or by the person who has been declared legally incompetent, within a month after the revocation of the declaration by the court.

177. The Capacity and Guardianship Law restricts the right of avoidance by providing two exceptions to this right. The first exception relates to a contract made by the minor, which is of a kind commonly made by minors of that age. The second exception relates to a contract made where one party is a minor or a person declared incompetent, and the other party neither knew nor ought to have known about it. However, these exceptions to the right of avoidance do not apply and the right remains in force, whenever the contract causes substantial harm to the minor, to the incompetent person, or to their property.

178. A special rule applies to 'credit-contracts', i.e., contracts that involve instalments and future-payments. Such contracts, extending money credit to minors, are void as long as the minor's representative has not given his consent in advance.

179. The Capacity and Guardianship Law, 1962, applies only to living persons. However, corporate or incorporate bodies in Israel may also have legal capacity to make contracts. The various enactments that deal with corporate bodies in private law grant them legal capacity. There are also enactments creating public corporations, which usually make such bodies capable of having rights and duties and of performing legal acts. The powers of all corporate bodies, whether their actions are governed by private or by public law, are limited in accordance with their defined goals. If they deviate from these goals, their action is considered '*ultra-vires*', and therefore void.

§2. Defects of Consent

180. Chapter 1 of the General Contracts Law, dealing with the making of a contract, examines the will of the parties entering a contract under the objective theory, which prefers the external indications of the agreement to the undisclosed intentions of the parties. Chapter 2 of the Law, dealing with defects in making a contract, deviates from this approach and gives weight and significance to the subjective will of the parties. Chapter 2 establishes a closed list of situations in which the free will and resolve of one of the parties was impaired, and therefore this party can rescind the contract.

I. Contract Concluded for Sake of Appearances

181. Section 13 of the General Contracts Law provides as follows:

> A contract made merely for appearance sake is void. This provision shall not affect a right acquired by a third party in *bona fide* reliance on the existence of a contract.

182. Section 13 differs from the other sections in Chapter 2. Unlike the sections that follow it, establishing grounds for rescinding a contract, section 13 does not establish grounds for the rescission of a contract but rather determines that a contract concluded for the sake of appearances is essentially void. A contract is deemed to be 'for appearance sake' when, by mutual agreement, it does not express the true intent of the parties. In European legal traditions this kind of a contract is named *simulation.*

183. Since section 13 does not provide for the rescission of the contract but rather views the contract as void *ab initio*, sections 19 and 21 of the General Contracts Law, which respectively concern partial rescission and restitution after rescission, do not apply. The obligation of restitution in this case originates from the Unjust Enrichment Law.

184. The second part of section 13 protects the interest of a third party, who relied on a contract with good faith and was unaware that it was formed merely for the sake of appearance. This third party will be entitled to retain purchases made in reliance on the existence of a contract.

II. Mistake

A. *The Meaning of Mistake*

185. The law relating to mistake is governed by the provisions of section 14 of the General Contracts Law, which provides as follows:

(a) Where a person has entered into a contract in consequence of a mistake and it may be assumed that but for the mistake he would not have entered into it, and the other party knows or should have known this, he may rescind the contract.
(b) Where a person has entered into a contract in consequence of a mistake and it may be assumed that but for the mistake he would not have entered into it, but the other party did not know and need not have known this, the Court may, on the application of the party who was mistaken, rescind the contract if it considers it just to do so. Upon doing so, the court may require the party who was mistaken to pay compensation for the damage caused to the other party in consequence of the formation of the contract.
(c) A mistake is not a ground for recission of the contract under this section if the contract can be preserved by rectifying the mistake and the other party, before the contract has been rescinded, gives notice that he is prepared to rectify it.
(d) For the purposes of this section and of section 15, 'mistake' means a mistake of fact or of law, but does not include a mistake as to the expediency of the transaction.

186. While section 14 does not contain a definition of 'mistake', the term has been interpreted by the courts as implying a thought or belief on the part of the mistaken party, which fails to correspond to reality.[51] The legislator's preference for theoretical simplicity and uniformity of approach is evidenced by the abandonment of fine distinctions between different kinds of mistakes. Section 14(d), for example, expressly eliminates the traditional distinction drawn by English law between mistake of fact and mistake of law. The distinction between mistake of fact and mistake of law was discarded following decisions in which this distinction had been criticized and recommendations made that it be abolished.[52]

187. According to section 14(d), a mistake that relates solely to the expediency of the transaction does not constitute an operative mistake. Such mistakes, which

51. *Rabinowitz v. Shelev* (1986) 40(4) PD 533, 541.
52. For example, *Japhet v. Eastwood* (1969) 23(1) PD 604, 613.

relate to the anticipated commercial or economic value of the transaction, may amount to no more than poor predictions as to the future. Clearly, failure to exclude them from the scope of the law would undermine the security of commercial transactions. Nonetheless, a mistake as to expediency of the transaction, which originates from a mistake concerning other assumptions related to the transaction, e.g., the quality of the purchased goods or the identity of the other party, can constitute an operative mistake. Similarly, a mistake as to motive stemming from false assumptions, other than those related to the expediency of the transaction, can also be recognized as an effective mistake.

B. Mistake Known to the Other Party

188. The pivotal distinction drawn in section 14 is the one between mistakes known to the other party (section 14(a)) and mistakes which are not known to the other party (section 14(b)). In both cases, however, the mistaken party, seeking to rescind the contract, must establish the following three elements.

189. First, that a valid, albeit defective, contract was in fact concluded between the parties. Hence, cases of mutual mistake, in which offer and acceptance fail to coincide, are governed by the rules of formation of a contract, and not by those concerning mistake.

190. Second, that the mistaken party entered into the contract 'in consequence of the mistake'. The test for establishing the required causal connection is a subjective one concerning the mistaken party's mental state.

191. Third, that the mistake was of a fundamental character, relating to the root and essence of the transaction. This requirement is implicit in the words of section 14(a) and (b): 'and it may be assumed that but for the mistake he would not have entered into it' (namely into the contract). The test of this element is an objective one, requiring the mistaken party to establish the reasonableness of the assumption that but for the mistake he would not have entered into the contract.

192. Having established the above elements, the mistaken party will have an immediate and absolute right to rescind the contract, providing that the other party knew or should have known of the mistake (section 14(a)). The extent of knowledge required is that of a reasonable man, placed in the same circumstances. The mistaken party will usually find it easier to establish such assumed or constructive knowledge (the other party 'should have known') than actual knowledge (the other party 'knew').

193. However, the moral and economic justification for entitling the mistaken party to rescind the contract is based on the other party's actual knowledge. Morally, where the other party knows of the mistake but does not point it out to the mistaken party, he should not be entitled to benefit from the contract. Economically, the party who knows of the mistake is in the best position to prevent it, thereby avoiding a waste of resources to both the mistaken party and society as a whole.

C. Mistake Not Known to the Other Party

194. In the absence of actual or constructive knowledge of the mistake, the other party has a strong claim for protection. This aim is achieved in section 14(b) by requiring the mistaken party to apply to the court for rescission. Moreover, the court may rescind the contract only 'if it considers it just so to do' having regard for all the relevant circumstances of the case.

195. In applying its power and the test of justice embodied in section 14(b), the court will take into account the interests of both parties: the mistaken and the non-mistaken. The court will attempt to determine whether the injustice caused to the mistaken party, should he remain bound by the contract, would outweigh the injustice caused to the other party by rescission.

196. Where the court decides to rescind the contract, then, according to section 14(b), 'Upon doing so, the court may require the party who was mistaken to pay compensation for the damage caused to the other party in consequence of the formation of the contract.' Presumably, such compensation will extend only to negative damages. The possibility of safeguarding the other party's interests through the mechanism of compensation will be one of the factors considered by the court in deciding whether to rescind the contract.

D. Rectification

197. Section 14(c) enables the other party to avoid rescission by rectifying the mistake if the contract can be preserved by such rectification, and if the party gives notice that it is prepared to rectify it before the contract is rescinded.

198. It follows that in cases where the mistaken party is entitled to rescind the contract, that party may also be able to thwart the possibility of rectification. He or she may do so by giving a notice of rescission to the other party before the latter has been able to give notice of its willingness to rectify. In such cases the mistaken party is, in effect, entitled to choose between rescission and rectification. This right, however, must be viewed as subject to the general principle of Israeli contract law requiring that rights be exercised in customary manner and in good faith.[53]

53. Discussed above at paras 71–82.

E. Clerical Error

199. Section 16 of the General Contracts Law provides as follows:

> Where a clerical or similar error has occurred in a contract, the contract shall be rectified in accordance with the presumed intention of the parties and the error shall not be a ground for rescission of the contract.

200. A clerical error involves an error in the written expression of the agreement. As such, it is not a genuine mistake. Instead, it is assumed that the parties have reached an agreement with no mistakes, the only problem being an improper expression in the written document.

III. Deceit (Misrepresentation)

201. Section 15 of the General Contracts Law provides as follows:

> A person who has entered into a contract in consequence of a mistake resulting from deceit practised upon him by the other party or a person acting on his behalf may rescind the contract. For this purpose, 'deceit' includes the non-disclosure of facts which according to law, custom or the circumstances the other party should have disclosed.

202. The deceit referred to in section 15 will generally take the form of a false, verbal, pre-contractual declaration, not being part of the written contract, and referring to some present or past fact or state of affairs. However, difficult problems may arise when it is claimed that such a declaration was included in the contract as one of its actual terms. In such cases the dispute will be settled objectively: not with reference to the intentions of the parties, but rather to their conduct, relative positions, oral statements and other relevant circumstances.

203. As in the case of mistake, rescission on grounds of deceit involves the assumption that a valid contract was made. In addition, the party seeking rescission must establish the existence of a double causal connection, namely, between the deceit practiced upon him and the mistake, and between the mistake and the entry into the contract. In both cases, the causal connection is to be determined by a subjective test.

204. The mistake referred to in section 15, like that of section 14, may be of fact or of law, but not one as to the expediency of the transaction. Therefore, false words of praise by the seller of goods concerning his product will not entitle the buyer to rescind on grounds of deceit. In such cases the buyer may be entitled to compensation for breach of the duty to act in good faith in the pre-contractual negotiations.[54]

205. Unlike a mistake under section 14, however, the mistake caused by deceit need not be of a fundamental character. It is not necessary for the deceived party to show that if not for the mistake induced by the deceit, a reasonable person would not have entered into the contract. Instead, the mistaken party must show that the mistake was caused by the deceit. The basic concept underlying section 15 is that the deceived party is entitled to a relative advantage since his manifestation of assent was induced by deceit practised upon him by the other party. Therefore, having established the required causal nexus between the deceit and the mistake, the party is exempt from further showing that the mistake was of a fundamental character.

206. Section 15 makes no provision for rectification of a mistake caused by deceit, even in those cases where the deceit is not indicative of any morally questionable conduct on the part of the party responsible for it. However, insistence on rescission, in spite of the deceiving party's willingness to rectify the mistake, may be considered as a breach of the obligation to exercise rights in good faith.[55]

207. According to section 15, deceit may be practised upon the deceived party 'by the other party or by a person acting on his behalf'. The latter is a physical or legal entity, separate from the other party to the contract, acting in its name or pursuant to his instructions.

208. Deceit is defined in section 15 as including non-disclosure. Hence, deceit can result from either an act, an omission or a combination of the two, as when a person, responding to a question concerning the state of his assets, fails to mention the existence of a lien on them. The obligation concerning disclosure is directly opposed to the *caveat emptor* approach of English law and is one of the manifestations of the governing principle of good faith.

209. Disclosure is required of facts which 'according to law, custom or the circumstances the party should have disclosed'.

210. A number of specific, statutory provisions in Israeli law create a duty of disclosure of facts which 'according to law' the contracting party should have disclosed.[56]

---

54. Discussed above at paras 143 et seq.
55. Discussed above at paras 71 et seq.
56. To give but one example, s. 16 of the Sale Law, 1968, provides: 'If the non-conformity arises out of facts which the seller knew or should have known when the contract was concluded and which he did not disclose to the buyer, the buyer is entitled to rely on it notwithstanding the provisions of section 14 and 15 or of any agreement, provided that he will give notice of it to the seller immediately upon discovering it.'

211. The reference to 'custom' in section 15 is meant to apply to cases in which parties will disclose material facts, as a matter of standard practice, prior to entering into a contract of the kind in question. Hence, section 15 gives such customs the force of law, so that they become legally binding on the parties.

212. The term 'circumstances' in section 15 refers to the specific, factual circumstances of the particular transaction. While the boundaries of this source of the obligation of disclosure are wider than those of the obligation according to law or custom, they are also less defined, and will depend on the facts of each particular case.

213. Failure to disclose material facts in the course of negotiations may entitle the injured party not only to rescind the resulting contract pursuant to section 15 but also to sue for compensation pursuant to section 12(b).[57]

214. Section 15 does not include a requirement as to the state of mind of the deceiving party. Hence, assuming the other elements required by the section are established, a contract will be voidable on grounds of deceit where the deceiving party acted intentionally, rashly, negligently, or even innocently and in good faith. In this sense, the concept of deceit, as used in section 15, does not necessarily involve morally questionable conduct on the part of the deceiving party.

IV. Duress (Improper Pressure)

215. Section 17(a) of the General Contracts Law provides as follows:

> A person who has entered into a contract in consequence of duress, by force or threats applied to him by the other party or a person acting on his behalf may rescind the contract.

216. In order to be entitled to rescind a contract on grounds of duress a party to the contract must be able to establish three separate elements, namely:

(1) the existence of a valid contract;
(2) duress; and
(3) a causal link between the fact of entrance into the contract and the duress applied, either by the other party to the contract or by a person acting to the latter's behalf.

217. The underlying assumption of section 17, which applies only where a valid (although defective) contract has been formed, is that the duress applied to the victim has not entirely negated his or her will and freedom of choice. However, the result of the duress is to severely reduce the victim's practical options so that he or

57. For further discussion, *see* paras 164–171.

she is forced to choose between the lesser of two evils. For this reason, a contract that has been entered in consequence of duress, though not void *ab initio*, is voidable and may be rescinded by the victim of the duress. In this respect, the approach of Israeli law is similar to that adopted by the classic continental tradition.

218. In resemblance to section 15 and unlike section 14, there is no requirement for the duress to be fundamental. It is unnecessary for the party claiming duress to show that but for the duress, he or she would not have entered the contract.

219. Section 17(a) expressly refers to duress either by force or by threats. Usually duress by force will be behavioural, while duress by threats will be verbal. In a verbal duress the other party indicates, orally or in writing, the dire consequences which will result if a contract is not made. Duress may amount to a tort or a criminal offence.[58]

220. The term 'duress', in the contractual context, should, however, be interpreted widely, so as to encompass any (unlawful) harm to a person's body, assets, liberty, social or economic position, which forces the victim to enter into the contract. This approach derives from the aim of section 17, which is to remedy defects in the victim's will, regardless of the kind of harm causing the defect.

221. Israeli courts have recognized that duress extends to economic duress as well.[59] Economic duress will exist when a party enters into a contract in order to free itself from unlawful business-like or commercial pressure exerted on him. Economic duress is subject to two tests: the quality and the intensity of the economic duress. The quality of the economic duress must be incompatible with standard commerce; the intensity of the economic duress must be such that the claimant party had no possible alternative, including an appeal to court.[60]

222. In contrast to both American and Continental systems, the provisions of section 17 recognize duress as a cause of rescission only if applied by the other party to the contract or by a person acting on his behalf. Hence, a contract will not be voidable where duress was applied by a third party not acting on behalf of the other party to the contract. This limitation indicates concern not only with the harm caused to the victim's will but also with the interests of the other party to the contract as well as with the demands of commerce and the dynamics of business life.

223. The causal link between the duress and the formation of the contract is determined by a subjective test. The party seeking to rescind the contract must show that the duress applied was such as to influence his or her will, and that but for the duress he or she (although not necessarily the reasonable individual placed is similar circumstances) would not have entered the contract.

---

58. *Supergas v. Mizrachi* (1958) 12 PD 394, 402.
59. *Shaul Rachamim Ltd. v. Expomedia Ltd.* (1989) 43(4) PD 95.
60. *Maya v. Panford* (1994) 48(5) 705.

224. Section 17(b) provides as follows:

> A *bona fide* warning of the exercise of a right does not constitute a threat for the purposes of this section.

225. The bona fide required by this subsection relates both to the existence of the right and to the means of its exercise. A warning to exercise a non-existing right will constitute duress unless the other party sincerely believes that it has the right in question. The warning must also relate to a means of exercising the right, which is both lawful and customary. A threat to initiate criminal proceedings in order to exercise a civil right will not necessarily lack bona fides.[61]

V. Extortion (Gross Disparity)

226. Section 18 of the General Contracts Law provides as follows:

> Where a person has entered into a contract in consequence of the other party or a person acting on his behalf, taking advantage of his distress, mental or physical weakness or inexperience, and the terms of the contract are less favourable to an unreasonable degree than is customary, he may rescind the contract.

227. Under Israeli penal law, extortion is also a criminal offence. In fact, the formulation of section 18 was copied, almost literally, from section 431 of the Penal Law, which had itself been adopted from German civil law.[62] Hence, the law relating to extortion has undergone a double metamorphosis: from (German) civil law to (Israeli) penal law; then, from (Israeli) penal law to (Israeli) civil law.

228. Prior to the enactment of section 18, and the recognition of extortion as grounds of rescission, the closest doctrine applied by Israeli courts in cases of extortion was that of undue influence. However, extortion should not be perceived as a mere substitute for undue influence. While both doctrines express similar moral and social ideas, extortion, as grounds of rescission, is to be interpreted independently and in accordance with the statutory elements which comprise it.

229. Unlike the other causes of rescission governed by the provisions of Chapter 2 of the General Contracts Law (i.e., mistake, deceit and duress), the assumption underlying section 18 is that the contract in question reflects the free will and resolve of the parties. Nevertheless, the circumstances referred to by section 18 are such as to justify, on grounds of morality and social justice, the rescission of the contract.

---

61. *Shappir v. Apple* (1985) 39(4) PD 149, 158.
62. *See* s. 138(2) of the B.G.B. However, under German law, extortion in the contractual context is not treated as a defect in the formation of a contract, but rather as leading to an immoral contract, which will be void *ab initio* and not merely voidable.

230. As in the cases of mistake, deceit and duress, the right to rescind on grounds of extortion assumes that a valid contract has been formed, and requires, *inter alia*, the existence of a causal connection between the extortion and the formation of the contract.

231. Extortion, as defined in section 18, is the exploitation of a person's distress, mental or physical weakness or inexperience. The terms 'extortion' and 'exploitation' connote immoral or unjust conduct. Therefore, it seems that the extorter must be aware of the other person's condition. Mere negligence on the extorter's part is insufficient. On the other hand, there is no requirement that the extorter be the one that caused the other party's mental or physical condition.

232. In light of the importance of the declared will of the parties and the protection of commercial transaction, a contract will be voidable on grounds of extortion only in extreme case of severe distress, mental or physical weakness or inexperience.

233. 'Distress', in the context of section 18, goes beyond a situation of poverty or the difficulties involved in dealing with economic problems. The term 'distress' refers to an abrupt change, leading to severe economic or psychological pressure at the time of the formation of the contract.

234. The term 'mental or physical weakness' in section 18 is broader than either mental or physical illness, and does not require that the contracting party's condition be such as to vitiate his or her legal capacity. However, a mere lack of understanding, or a disparity in the parties' respective levels of education, will not suffice.

235. The 'inexperience' of the party must be such as to extend beyond a mere lack of business sense or expertise concerning the details of the transaction. It must amount to a general characteristic of the person, deriving from limitations in his or her social or educational background.

236. Even where the causal connection between extortion and the formation of the contract has been established, the contract will be voidable only if 'the terms of the contract are less favourable to an unreasonable degree than is customary'. This requirement is determined by an objective test. Customary terms are those terms which are in actual use and appear frequently in contracts of the kind in question. Where the contract is not of an ordinary kind, thus leaving no such external criteria as to what constitutes customary terms, the court will fill the gap by using a theoretical standard, based on the court's view as to what is just and fair in a relationship such as the one between the parties.[63]

63. *See, e.g.*, the decision in *Hotel Eden Nahariya v. Kassel* (2014), where the court compared the contract under discussion to a previous contract between the parties.

237. In comparing the actual terms of the contract to the customary terms, the court will take into account a wide range of circumstances, including market conditions and the relative bargaining positions of the parties to the contract. This comparison allows the court to determine whether the contract is, to an unreasonable degree, less favourable than is customary.

§3. Other Conditions of Validity

I. Illegality

238. Section 30 of the General Contracts Law provides:

> A contract the making, contents or object of which is or are illegal, immoral or contrary to public policy is void.

239. In accordance with the above provision an illegal contract is one where the making, contents or object of which is or are contrary to the law. In order to add substance to this definition, distinctions have been drawn in case law between mandatory provisions of a law and those which are merely discretionary, it being held that only those contracts which contravene the former will be deemed illegal. A further distinction is between essential and merely incidental illegality. However, these distinctions have not been useful in interpreting a statutory provision in order to determine whether a contract in contravention thereof is illegal. The question of illegality of a contract is indeed a matter of interpretation of the statute. The Supreme Court has posed the question of illegality as follows: would invalidating a contract contravening a statutory prohibition achieve the statue's purpose, or is the statutory sanction accompanying the prohibition sufficient in itself for furthering the purpose of the statue in question.[64]

240. The line between the three categories by virtue of which a contract may be illegal, namely the making, contents or object thereof, is not always easy to draw. In many cases, like in the case of a contract for the commission of a criminal offence, the contract is illegal in all three categories.

241. The making of a particular contract will be illegal where the actual stage of the making of the contract is by itself tainted by illegality. This will be the case where the contract is made in contravention of the provisions of a specific law, as when, for example, a local authority makes a contract without first issuing the tender required by law.

242. The object of the contract is the object of the parties to the contract. However, where the illegal object is that of only one of the parties, it will suffice if the other party, knowing of the illegal object, agreed to make the contract. The object

64. *Albert Zaguri v. National Labour Court* (1992) 49(4) PD 749.

of the contract is determined by the intentions of the parties at the time the contract was made. Hence, the fact that subsequently the object is not achieved will not remedy the invalidity of the contract.

243. A contract the object of which is to defraud the tax authorities by specifying false sums is an illegal contract. However, it was held that the fact that sums specified in the contract are different from those actually agreed upon by the parties is, in itself, insufficient to invalidate the contract.[65] The party claiming illegality must adduce additional evidence regarding the fact that the aim of the discrepancy was to evade the payment of tax.[66]

244. An agreement by the parties to perform a contract in an illegal manner, whether such agreement was reached prior to the conclusion of the contract or after the contract was made, will deem the contract an illegal one. Similarly, performance, which was legal at the time the contract was made but became illegal thereafter, will also fall within the scope of section 30.[67]

II. Public Policy

245. Section 30 of the General Contracts Law invalidates, besides illegal contracts, contracts 'the making, contents or objects of which are...immoral or contrary to public policy'.

246. Although section 30 refers to immorality as a separate ground of invalidity, the accepted view is that this category can be comprised within the scope of public policy and is thus superfluous.

247. Public policy is perceived by Israeli jurisprudence as a general judicial yardstick of which the significance, content and application are subject to the court's discretion. The concept is a dynamic one, reflecting both the fundamental notions of the Israeli legal system and the prevalent moral, social and economic views.

248. Israeli courts are reluctant to declare a contract void on grounds of public policy except for the most extreme cases, where the contract undermines the very foundations of the social order. This reluctance stems from two sources: first, the inevitable clash between the provision of section 30 and the rule that validity should be given to agreements which the parties freely undertook; second, the ambiguity inherent in the concept of public policy.

249. In spite of the courts' reluctance to declare contracts as contrary to public policy, there is a category of contracts that must pass the test of public policy, and these are contracts in restraint of trade. According to the doctrine of restraint of

65. *Chevrat Tirat Gush* 6195 *v. Tom Tov Levi* (1977) 31(2) PD 334.
66. *Shaltiel v. Shani* (1981) 36(2) PD 151.
67. *Amidar—National Co for Immigrant Housing Ltd v. Hai* (2010) 63 (3) PD 795.

trade, a contractual obligation restraining one of the parties' freedom of occupation, can be deemed as contrary to public policy and therefore void. The doctrine of restraint of trade recognizes two main types of restrictions on the freedom of trade: first, an obligation limiting the right of the employee to compete with his employer at some future date; second, an obligation undertaken by the seller of a business, restricting him from engaging in a similar business in the future. Israeli case law has shown willingness to interfere more readily in the case of the first type of obligations as opposed to the second type. The reason generally cited for this difference of attitude is the usual lack of equality in the respective positions of the parties to a contract of employment.

§4. The Consequences of a Defect of Consent or of a Lack of Substantive Validity

I. Defect of Consent

A. *Voidability*

250. Defects of consent result in the contract being voidable, not void. Therefore, unless and until the party entitled to rescind elects to do so, the contract will be valid. The right or power to rescind in such circumstances derives from the principle of freedom of contract: just as a party should be free to contract in accordance with its free will, it should also be free to rescind a contract where such will has been defective. The right of rescission, like all rights under Israeli law, must be exercised in customary manner and in good faith.[68]

B. *Partial Rescission*

251. Section 19 of the General Contracts Law provides as follows:

> Where the contract is severable and the ground for rescission relates only to one part thereof, such part alone shall be capable of rescission. But if it is to be assumed that the party entitled to rescind would not have entered into the contract but for that ground, he may either rescind the said part or the whole contract.

252. The first part of the above provision constitutes an exception to the general rule which stipulates that defects of consent entitle the injured party to rescind the contract as a whole; the second part constitutes an exception to this exception.

68. This result may be reached either directly by viewing the right of rescission as a 'right arising out of a contract' which, according to s. 39 of the General Contracts Law, must be exercised in customary manner and in good faith, or, by means of s. 61(b) of the Law, which applies the provisions of the Law, including those of s. 39, to 'legal acts other than contracts', including the rescission of a contract by reason of a defect of consent.

253. The party wishing to limit the rescission to a partial one must establish both that the contract is severable and that grounds for rescission relate only to one part thereof. The question whether a particular contract is severable requires interpretation of the contract and will be resolved by reference to the specific context and circumstances of the case. Nevertheless, certain guidelines for determining this issue can be discerned. A contract will be severable only if it comprises separate 'contractual units' composed of mutual obligations attributable to each other. Even more so, a contract will not be severable where this would either injure the independence of the severed part or detract from the value of the remaining parts of the contract.

254. Even where the two conditions of partial rescission have been established, the party entitled to rescind will have the option of choosing between partial rescission and rescission of the whole contract, if it can be assumed that this party would not have entered the contract but for the grounds for its rescission. Within this context the test will be an objective one, regardless of whether the said grounds relate to mistake, deceit, duress or extortion.

C. Mode of Rescission

255. Section 20 of the General Contracts Law provides as follows:

> Rescission of a contract shall be by notice by one party to the other party given within a reasonable time after becoming aware of the ground for rescission or, in the case of duress, within a reasonable time after becoming aware that the duress has ceased.

256. With the exception of a mistake not known to the other party, the right to rescind by reason of a defect of consent is an autonomous right, exercisable by means of 'notice by one party to the other party'. Such notice is both a necessary condition and an element of the rescission. Rescission occurs with the notification – and not with the delivery – of the rescission. In order to become valid, the notice must satisfy certain conditions relating to form, content and time.

257. Regarding the form of the notice reference should be made to section 60(a) of the General Contracts Law, which provides as follows:

> Notice under this Law shall be given in the manner customary in the circumstances of the case.

258. Although section 20 does not stipulate any specific demands relating to form, the notice must emanate from the party entitled to rescind and must be directed to the other party. Such requirements will, however, be subject to the principle of good faith so that a party may not be able to take advantage of the fact that the content of the notice which has become known to him, was not directed to him.

259. The content of the notice must express the party's intention to terminate the contractual relations between the parties in a clear and unambiguous manner. However, the notice need not be formally expressed: conduct from which the intention to rescind can be clearly inferred may suffice. The actual submission of a statement of claims demanding damages and restitution following rescission may constitute adequate notice of rescission.[69]

260. Notice must be given by the party seeking rescission within reasonable time after becoming aware of the ground for rescission; otherwise, the notice will have no effect and the contract, although defective, will remain valid. The question whether this condition has been satisfied will be determined objectively by the courts, having regard to all the relevant circumstances of the particular case. For the purposes of section 20 the party entitled to rescind must first have actual knowledge of the ground for rescission: constructive knowledge will not suffice.

261. According to the second part of section 20, cited above, in the case of duress – and only in this case – the lapse of reasonable time is determined as the lapse of reasonable time since the party seeking rescission becomes aware that the duress has ceased. The reason for this special provision is that the effect of the duress, which caused the party to enter the contract, may continue so as to also prevent him from rescinding. Hence, it is only after the party has become aware that duress has ceased that he will be able to exercise his right of rescission.

D. Consequences of Rescission

262. The rescission of the contract will have implications both for the relations of the parties to the contract *inter se* and for their relations to third parties. With regard to third parties, the accepted view is that an acquisition by a third party in bona fide reliance on the defective contract will be protected only if made in good faith and for consideration.

263. With regard to the implications of rescission between the parties to the contract, the general rule is that rescission will discharge the parties from all future obligations arising under the contract. However, certain stipulations – such as those relating to arbitration or agreed compensation – will continue to bind the parties even after rescission.

264. Of special importance are the provisions relating to restitution in section 21 of the Law:

> Where a contract has been rescinded, each party shall restore to the other party what he has received under the contract or, if restitution is impossible or unreasonable, pay him the value of what he has received.

69. *Rabinowitz v. Shelev* (1986) 40(4) PD 533, 545.

265. As the opening words of this provision clearly indicate, rescission of the contract is a prerequisite condition of restitution. Following rescission, the obligation to make restitution is mutual and lies equally on both parties: each party must restore to the other what it has received under the contract (or value thereof), and each party is entitled to receive from the other whatever was given under the contract (or value thereof). The right of restitution is an obligatory rather than a proprietary right. The theoretical basis of the obligation to make restitution lies in the law of unjust enrichment, the aim of restitution being to prevent the unjust enrichment of one party at the expense of the other.

266. Restitution will be impossible in the case of an asset which has been lost, destroyed, consumed or acquired by a third party, as well as in the case of work which has been performed or a service which has been rendered. Restitution of an asset that has lost its original form as a result of having been mixed with, or attached to, other objects, is unreasonable. In these cases, the obligation will be to pay the value of what has been received under the contract.

267. In accordance with the law of unjust enrichment, where money is being restored, restitution will include interest, as well as index differentials.

II. Lack of Substantive Validity

268. As mentioned above, according to section 30 of the General Contracts Law, 'A contract the making, contents or object of which is or are illegal, immoral or contrary to public policy is void.' This section must, however, be read in conjunction with section 31 of the Law which deals with the consequences of such invalid contracts.

269. The first part of section 31 provides as follows:

> The provisions of sections 19 and 21 shall apply *mutatis mutandis* to the avoidance of a contract under this chapter … .

270. Section 19 deals with partial rescission.[70] In applying section 19 to invalid contracts in accordance with section 31, the court – not the parties to the contract – is permitted to declare avoidance of the entire contract, or declare partial avoidance. In considering partial avoidance the court will generally proceed in stages: first, whether the contract is severable, second, whether the ground for avoidance relates only to one part thereof and, third, whether it is possible to isolate the tainted part from the remainder without thereby producing a meaningless contract, or one different from that which the parties entered. Where the level of illegality, or the degree to which the contract is contrary to public policy, is severe, the whole contract will be tainted and thus void.

70. Discussed above at paras 251–254.

271. The provisions of section 21 deal with restitution.[71] Applying these provisions – *mutatis mutandis* – via section 31, to invalid contracts, represents a significant innovation within Israeli law. Today, contrary to the traditional position of English law concerning illegal contracts, the invalidity of a contract no longer constitutes a barrier to a claim for restitution. Restitution has become the general rule and the principal remedy in such cases. Illegal contracts are – in principle and subject to the special powers granted to the court in section 31 – devoid of any consequences and cannot transfer property rights.

272. The second part of section 31 provides as follows:

> Provided that in the case of avoidance under section 30 the court may, if it deems it just so to do and on such conditions as it sees fit, relieve a party of the whole or part of the duty under section 21 and, in so far as one party has fulfilled his obligation under the contract, require the other party to fulfil the whole or part of the corresponding obligation.

273. The second part of section 31 grants the court two exceptional powers concerning illegal contracts that are void according to section 30: the power to relieve a party from its obligation to make restitution and the power to require it to fulfil its corresponding obligation under the contract. In fact, in both cases the court will give effect to the valid transfer of property rights despite the invalidity of the contract.

274. The court will exercise its powers under section 31 'only if it deems it just so to do'. The concept of justice within this context is a relative one, understood as referring primarily to the balancing of interests between the parties to the contract. In exercising these powers, the court will determine each particular case on grounds of its own facts, taking into account all relevant circumstances. Such circumstances include, *inter alia*, the terms of the contract, the respective conduct of the parties, especially of the party bringing the suit, the interests of bona fide third-party purchasers, the degree of illegality or immorality of the contract and the degree to which the contract has already been performed. The court may also be influenced by wider, social considerations, like the need to foster a sense of public respect for the law.

275. The power to relieve a party of its obligation to make restitution constitutes an exception to the general rule requiring restitution; as such, this power will be construed narrowly and exercised only if the court is convinced that justice cannot be served by restitution. When restitution is claimed, the court will consider the purpose for which the money or asset was given. Hence, the court will reject a claim for restitution of money paid as a bribe or in return for a promise to commit an offence.

---

71. Discussed above at paras 264–267.

276. In requiring a party to fulfil the whole or part of an obligation under the contract, the court is not enforcing the invalid contract, but only ordering the fulfilment of a corresponding obligation where the other party has already fulfilled its own obligation or a substantial part thereof. This power will also be construed narrowly and exercised only if the court deems it just to do so.

277. The accepted view is that the court may not exercise its power to order fulfilment of a corresponding obligation to award the plaintiff the remedy of compensation in general or agreed compensation in particular.

Chapter 3. The Contents of a Contract

§1. Interpretation

I. The Process

278. The interpretation of a contract may be regarded as the intellectual process whereby the contract's boundaries are demarcated, and the scope of its obligations is determined. The interpretation of a contract determines its meaning, and thus its validity and consequences.

279. In interpreting and thereby understanding a contract, the court aims to determine and clarify the intention of the parties by reconstructing their thoughts at the time the contract was made.

II. Interpretation According to the Intention of the Parties

280. At present, the main Israeli rule of contractual interpretation is stipulated in section 25(a) of the General Contracts Law:

> A contract shall be interpreted in accordance with the presumed intention of the parties as it appears there-from and as appearing from the circumstances. However, if the intention of the parties is clearly implied from the language of the contract, the contract shall be interpreted according to its language.

281. The test applied is an objective test of reasonableness: The intention of the parties, who are assumed to be reasonable, is determined objectively in accordance with the language of the contract and the circumstances of the case. Moreover, the intention in question is the common intention of both parties rather than the subjective intention of one of them.

282. Prior to 2011, section 25(a) provided:

> A contract shall be interpreted in accordance with the intention of the parties as appearing therefrom or, in so far as it does not so appear, as appearing from the circumstances.

283. In the past, in applying this section, the Israeli courts used the 'two-stage technique' when interpreting a contract. According to this technique, the courts first referred to the written contract, and only when its language was unclear or ambiguous they resorted to its interpretation according to surrounding circumstances at the time the contract was made. This was the legal state of affairs until 1995, the year Former Chief Justice Barak delivered his landmark decision in the famous *Aprofim* case.[72]

284. In this case, the orthodox approach of interpretation in two stages was replaced by a new approach, namely a teleological or purposive approach, typical of Former Chief Justice Barak's general interpretation theory. This new approach establishes the purpose of the contract as the main source of interpretation.[73]

285. Under to the purposive interpretation approach, ascertaining the original intention of the parties from the clear language of the contract marks the starting point of the interpretation process, but not its end.

286. Interpretation of the contract entails a one-stage test, involving a continuous movement from the language of the contract to its external circumstances. The purposive interpretation theory enables the parties to present to the court a broad and comprehensive body of factual evidence at the early stage of the interpretation process.

287. The *Aprofim* case also enhances the importance of the principle of good faith in the interpretation process. According to the new interpretive approach applied in this case, the interpretation of a contract must be done in a way that conforms to its purpose. When the parties' common intention is unknown, the court can complete the contract by utilizing the principle of good faith.

288. The *Aprofim* ruling was ratified ten years later, whereby an extended panel of judges determined that the purposive approach is the correct one for the interpretation of a contract.[74] This decision was followed by acute objections by some Supreme Court judges as well as by members of the legal community.

289. The above-mentioned dispute led to the amendment of section 25(a).[75] The legislator's initial intention in this rare amendment (the only substantive amendment to the General Contracts Law since its enactment) was to abolish the decision of *Aprofim* and to revert to the 'two-stage technique'. Yet the new syntax did not result in real change. Section 25(a) was interpreted by the Supreme Court as anchoring the *Aprofim* decision albeit with renewed emphasis on the language of the contract.[76]

290. In conclusion, a contract is interpreted in accordance with the contracting parties' intent as it appears from its language and from the external circumstances.

72. *The State of Israel v. Aprofim Housing and Enterprise* (1995) 49(2) PD 265.
73. For an analysis of Barak's purposive interpretation, *see* Gabriela Shalev, *Interpretation in Law – Chief Justice Barak's Theory*, in *Liber Amicorum Jacques Herbots* (Kluwer, 2002) and in 36(2002) Is.L.Rev. 123.
74. *The Vegetable Growers Association v. The State of Israel* (2006) 61(2) PD 1681.
75. Discussed above at paras 280 et seq.
76. *The National Insurance Institute v. Sahar* (2012).

However, the language of the contract is central. When, and only when, the intention of the contracting parties cannot be implied from the language and from the external circumstances of the contract, the court will turn to the good faith principle.

III. Interpretation Validating the Contract

291. Section 25(b) of the General Contracts Law provides as follows:

> Where a contract is capable of different interpretations, an interpretation preserving it is preferable to an interpretation according to which it is void.

292. The above rule will apply only if, after having interpreted the contract in accordance with the intention of the parties, the contract is still capable of sustaining two distinct, equally reasonable interpretations, one preserving the contract's validity, while according to the other the contract is void. In such circumstances, the interpreter, namely the court, is instructed to prefer the former interpretation.

293. The validating rule is based on the logical assumption that the parties intended to enter into a valid and effective contract. Hence, the desire to maintain the reasonable expectations of the parties leads, where possible, to the interpretation which preserves the contract's validity.

IV. Interpretation *'Contra Stipulatorem'*

294. Section 25(b1) of the General Contracts Law provides as follows:

> Where a contract is capable of different interpretations, and one of the parties had precedence over the other in the formulation of its terms, an interpretation against the formulating party is preferable to an interpretation in his favour.

295. Section 25(b1) was formulated as part of an amendment to the General Contracts Law in 2011. It establishes the *contra stipulatorem* rule. Before the amendment, this rule was applied by the court as part of the judge-made law or common law.

296. Section 25(b1) now stipulates that an ambiguity in the contract giving rise to two equal reasonable interpretations will be interpreted against the party who drafted the contract and in favour of the other party. The justification for this provision rests on the principle that a person is responsible for his or her actions.

297. As in the case of English law, from which the rule was adopted, Israeli courts had applied the rule primarily in the context of standard contracts (especially insurance contracts), where the party drafting the contract is usually also the stronger of the two parties to the transaction.

298. Section 25(b1) is broader than the *contra stipulatorem* rule and does not refer only to cases whereby the contract was entirely drafted by one of the parties, but also applies to situations where one of the parties had precedence in the formulation of the terms of the contract.

V. The Interpretation of Expressions and Stipulations

299. Section 25(c) of the General Contracts Law provides as follows:

> expressions and stipulations in a contract which are customarily used in contracts of that kind shall be interpreted in accordance with the meanings assigned to them in such contracts.

300. The above provision is based on the assumption that when parties to a contract of a certain kind make use of certain expressions and stipulations customarily used in contracts of that kind, they intend, in all likelihood, for such expressions and stipulations to be interpreted in accordance with the meanings assigned to them in such contracts. Hence, the rule of interpretation embodied in this provision derives from the intention of the parties and is, therefore, subject to their intention. For this reason, if a contrary intention is proved, it will take precedence over the assumption implicit in the statutory provision. However, in the absence of a contrary intention, the meanings customarily assigned to the expressions and stipulations employed by the parties will take precedence over their plain, literal meanings; for it is the former meanings which will be assumed to reflect the parties' intention.

VI. The Application of Provisions from the Interpretation Law, 1981

301. Section 25(d) of the General Contracts Law applies, *mutatis mutandis*, a number of auxiliary rules dealing with the interpretation of statutes, to the interpretation of contracts. This section has been criticized for importing hidden and almost inaccessible sections of law into substantive contract law, instead of including all relevant rules of contractual interpretation within the General Contracts Law itself.

302. In any case, section 25 establishes a hierarchic arrangement, so that the extrinsic statutory provisions applied via section 25(d) will be subject to the interpretation rules contained in the preceding subsections.

§2. The Different Clauses

I. Supplementation of the Contract

303. Section 26 of the General Contracts Law provides as follows:

'Particulars not determined by or under the contract shall be in accordance with the practice obtaining between the parties, or in the absence of such a practice, in accordance with the practice customary in contracts of that kind, and such particulars shall also be regarded as having been agreed'.

304. The process of ascertaining the terms of a contract may be divided into two distinct stages, the first being interpretation (discussed above) and the second being supplementation. Supplementation assumes the existence of a valid contract. Furthermore, supplementation takes place, if at all, only after the contract had first been interpreted in accordance with the provisions of section 25.

305. A contract can be supplemented by means of extrinsic sources, namely, the law and practice. Supplementation of essential terms is achieved by means of general or specific statutory provisions; particulars in a contract are supplemented by recourse to practice. The term 'particulars' in section 26 has been interpreted as referring to non-material aspects of the contract, which are only of secondary importance.[77]

306. Section 26 of the General Contracts Law deals with the supplementation of 'particulars', and provides that the process of supplementation is to be done, first, in accordance with the practice established between the parties and, in the absence of such a practice, in accordance with the customary practice concerning contracts of that kind. Hence, the process of supplementation, unlike that of interpretation, is not necessarily linked to the parties' actual intention. Since, as mentioned above, the term 'particulars' refers to aspects of the contract that are of secondary importance, section 26 does not enable the court to introduce significant or fundamental changes into the contract.

307. A contract may be supplemented pursuant to section 26 only with respect to particulars undetermined 'by or under' the contract. Hence, in order to be supplemented, the contract must contain a genuine gap or *lacuna*. Moreover, supplementation can take place only when the parties' silence with respect to a certain matter does not simply reflect a negative arrangement (namely, that the parties deliberately and intentionally did not address a certain matter), but actually requires supplementation. Particulars determined 'under' the contract involve, for example, particulars which can be ascertained by the application of external criteria, such as the consumer price index to be published at some future date. Arrangements of this kind constitute part of the contract, and where they exist there is no *lacuna* in need of supplementation.

308. The concept of a 'practice' refers to a form of conduct, which constitutes a common behaviour in a certain field (namely a usage), and it has no normative

77. *Martziano v. Ben Shoshan* (1976) 30(3) PD 729, 732–733.

aspect. Section 26 distinguishes between private and general practice. Private practice being the practice established between the parties while general practice being the practice customary in contracts of that kind. Where a private practice exists, it has priority over the general practice.

309. Practice customary in contracts of a certain kind, is the common and acceptable behaviour practiced between businesspersons within a specific field.[78] Reference may be made to general practices which did not exist at the time the contract between the parties was made, but were formed only later; for as mentioned above, the application of section 26, unlike that of section 25, is not necessarily linked to the actual intention or will of the parties.

310. Once a contract has been supplemented by recourse to practice, the supplemented particulars are regarded 'as having been agreed' upon, and as constituting part of the contract. In this sense, practices take precedence over statutory provisions, which are inserted into the contract only after the process of interpretation and of supplementation have been completed, and after it has been ascertained that the parties did not contract out of such provisions. The assumption underlying this approach is that practices are closer to the parties' intention and expectations than the relevant statutory provisions.

311. Like any other fact, the existence of a practice, whether private or general, must be proved. The proof of a general practice, however, requires a stronger evidentiary basis than the proof of a practice established between the parties. The burden of proof rests on the party claiming the existence of the practice. Practices may be proved by means of expert witnesses. Where the practice is a solid and well-known one, it may be possible to assume judicial knowledge thereof.

II. Interpretation and Supplementation in Accordance with the Principle of Good Faith

312. The principle of good faith is one of the most fundamental principles of Israeli contract law. According to the *Aprofim* ruling, supplementation, as well as interpretation, must be carried out in a way that corresponds with the contract's purpose.[79] Interpreting contracts in accordance with the principle of good faith requires the tracing of the parties' genuine intention. Filling *lacunae* and resolving ambiguities in the contract must also be done according to the principle of good faith, taking into account the purpose of the contracting parties.

---

78. *Chasid v. Prasot* (1985) 39(4) PD 451, 457–458.
79. Discussed above at paras 283–290.

III. Supplementation of the Contract for an Indefinite Period

313. The supplementation of a contract for an indefinite period has hitherto received a normative solution only in the provisions of the Lease and Lending Law, 1971 and the Insurance Contract Law, 1981. According to these provisions each party may terminate a lease or an insurance contract for an indefinite time by notifying the other party within reasonable time.

314. These provisions reflect the general attitude of the law against perpetual or eternal contracts. A contract that does not specify its period is not to last forever; it can be terminated by notice of each party, within reasonable time.

IV. Implied Terms

315. The purpose of the Common Law doctrine of implied terms is to fill gaps in a contract, a task now governed by the provisions of sections 25 (interpretation) and 26 (supplementation) of the General Contracts Law. These provisions rendered the doctrine of implied terms redundant, so that it no longer forms part of Israeli contract law. The provisions embodied in sections 25 and 26 establish an original and independent mechanism for analysing legal questions and determining the scope of the contract.

316. The doctrine of implied terms is fundamentally different from and inconsistent with the above provisions. While section 25(a) refers to the intention of the parties as reflected from the contract, the doctrine of implied terms refers to the impliedly inferred intention of the parties. According to section 25(a), the language and the surrounding circumstances of the contract must be examined in interpreting it. By contrast, under the common law doctrine of implied terms, logical conclusions are inferred in accordance with abstract, extrinsic tests, namely the test of the 'officious bystander' and the test based on business efficacy.

317. Section 26 also differs from the doctrine of implied terms in logic and contents. Section 26 refers to 'particulars', namely non-material aspects of the contract, which were not determined by or under the contract. In comparison, the doctrine of implied terms deals with the supplementation of essential and fundamental terms of the contract, terms which – in their absence – the contract is not enforceable.

318. In view of these differences, the Common Law doctrine of implied terms should not continue to apply in Israeli contract law, either directly or indirectly, via sections 25 and 26. However, the concept of an 'implied contract' can be of use to describe a contract that is inferred from the conduct of the parties.

V. Standard Terms and Exemption Clauses

A. *Exemption Clauses*

319. According to Israeli law, exemption clauses are subject to the application of the principles and rules of the General Contracts Law, as well as the Standard Contracts Law, 1982.

320. The Standard Contract Law, 1982, regulates exemption clauses as well as other clauses in standard contracts. As most exemption clauses are included in standard contracts, there is not much room left for the application of the General Contracts Law to exemption clauses.

321. Exemption clauses in regular (non-standard) contracts are governed by the doctrine of public policy, discussed above.[80] The application of this doctrine to exemption clauses in regular contracts is very rare. In regular, non-standard contracts, clauses exempting a party from financial liability are usually immune to judicial intervention. The parties to a regular commercial transaction may exempt themselves from such liability. Each party to a commercial contract may accept risks and take chances, and each party may also obtain insurance against contractual exemptions. Therefore, there is no public policy rule that justifies the court's intervention to annul exemption clauses in a regular commercial contract. Even clauses exempting from liability for bodily injury in a regular contract will usually be upheld. Public policy will not justify setting aside such exemption clauses when they are included in a contract wilfully entered into by both parties (e.g., contract for dangerous sports or dangerous occupations).

B. *The Standard Contracts Law, 1982*

322. The Standard Contracts Law, 1982 (hereinafter: the Law), repealed a former Standard Contract Law, of the year 1964. The legislation of the old Standard Contract Law in 1964 made Israel the first country in the western world (except for Italy that had certain relevant sections in the Italian Civil Code 1942) that attempted to solve the complicated problems of standard contract terms by way of legislation. This pioneering Law regulated standard contracts directly through legislation, and imposed a dual system of judicial and administrative control. However, the years that passed since the enactment of this Law revealed its weaknesses and the inapplicability of its provisions. The main reasons for disappointment concerning the Law were:

(a) suppliers did not apply to the Tribunal created by the law in order to approve their standard contracts;

80. Discussed above at paras 245–249.

(b) customers were not aware of their rights under the law, and therefore did not utilize it;
(c) The courts ignored and misinterpreted the provisions of the law.

323. The modifications and amendments of the Law stemmed from the lessons learned through the application (or rather, the lack of application) of the original version of the Law. The new Law also established a stronger conceptual framework. Like its predecessor, the new Law provides for a combined system of judicial and administrative control, simultaneously reinforcing the device of pre-screening of standard contracts in the Tribunal.

C. Main Features of the Standard Contracts Law

1. Clarifying and Simplifying the Former Law

324. The Law opens with a definition of its purpose. Section 1 provides as follows:

> The purpose of this law is to protect customers from unduly disadvantageous conditions of standard contracts.

325. A provision defining the purpose of the Law is rare in civil legislation. Yet this opening section can be attributed to the judicial application of the former Law. Although the former Standard Contracts Law, 1964, also empowered the court to invalidate prejudicial clauses in standard contracts, this Law was often ignored or misinterpreted. As a result, some of the court's decisions on standard contracts attracted academic criticism. The main fallacy in the court's attitude was the application of general contract rules, mainly those of public policy (but also those of insufficient notice and good faith), as criteria for repeal of disadvantageous conditions in standard contracts. Now that the Law's purpose has been clarified, the Law is applied in accordance with independent, economic criteria; the courts are clearly instructed by the new Law to concentrate on the fairness of the transaction and the protection of consumers.

326. By emphasizing the Law's purpose, together with the simplification of its provisions, the legislator intended to establish it as part of the consumer's protection codification (although the Law applies to 'customers', a term which is broader than 'consumers') and make it more accessible to the public at large and not only to the legal profession. A later amendment to the Law, legislated in 2014, provides that judgments and other decisions of the Tribunal, as well as the standard contracts to which such judgements and decisions refer, shall be published.

2. Widening the Scope of the Law

327. The new Law applies to every standard contract, to every general term and to every party.

a. To Every Standard Contract

328. Unlike the former law, which applied only to contracts made for the supply of a commodity or a service, section 2 of the new Law defines a standard contract in broad terms as:

> a contract, all or some of the conditions of which were determined in advance by one party, in order to serve as conditions of many contracts between him and persons undefined as to number or identity.

329. Thus, the Law definitely applies to all standard contracts made within the territory of Israel, regardless of their subject matter.

b. To Every General Term

330. The 1964 Law specified a list (*numerus clausus*) of restrictive terms, and only these terms were subject to judicial or to administrative review. According to the new Law every term in a standard contract is now under review (with the exception of terms specified by section 23). A general contract term is defined in the Law (section 2) as a term that is:

(a) fixed in advance by one party only;
(b) intended to be used in many future contracts;
(c) not subject to negotiation.

331. The authority of both the court and the Tribunal to interfere and invalidate every disadvantageous contractual term is the main innovation of the new Law. Since a basic element of a standard contract is that negotiations are not feasible, terms, which were specifically agreed upon, were removed from the scope of the Law. To such terms traditional contract doctrines continue to apply.

332. The topic of price was also removed from the scope of the Law by means of section 23(1) which states: ‘The provisions of this law shall not apply to a condition determining the monetary consideration to be paid by the customer’. The rationale underlying this section is that a price term is normally the most important term of any contract, and therefore the adhering party is usually well aware of it (Yet, when the price is grossly unfair other remedies are available, mainly that of extortion pursuant to section 18 of the General Contracts Law).

c. To Every Party

333. While the former Law applied only to 'suppliers' in the economic sense of the term, namely, the party who provides services or commodities, now the supplier means the party who offers the transaction and in fact drafts the text of the standard contract. Hence, the Law applies also to a strong party (a monopoly, or even the State) that receives services or goods, according to standard forms prepared by this party.

3. Establishing (or: Re-establishing) a Combined System of Control

334. The main feature of the new Law (as well as the former law) is the system of combined control established by it: judicial control and administrative control. Judicial control is exercised by the courts, while administrative control is placed in the hands of a Tribunal, established by the Law, i.e., a Standard Contracts Tribunal. Both bodies have power to invalidate or alter disadvantageous conditions in a standard contract.

D. Test of Control

335. The test of control is provided for by section 3 of the Law which provides as follows:

> A court and the Tribunal will, under the provisions of this law, annul or change any condition of a standard contract which, having regard to the totality of the contract's conditions and to other circumstances, involves an undue disadvantage to customers or an unfair advantage for the supplier, which is likely to lead to the customers' deprivation (any such condition hereinafter: unduly disadvantageous condition.

336. This test of control indicates the 'consumerist' orientation of the law, and it is in fact a test of reasonableness and fairness in the relationship of customers and suppliers.

337. Disadvantageous conditions are thus subject to annulment or modifications both by the court and by the Tribunal. Section 4 of the Law contains a presumption that certain terms in standard contracts are disadvantageous to customers, with the practical result that the burden of proving the contrary is imposed upon the supplier.

338. Generally speaking, terms which are subject to the above presumption can be categorized as follows:

(a) conditions which exclude or restrict, in an unreasonable way, the supplier's liability towards the customer;
(b) conditions which confer upon the supplier the right to change in an unreasonable way essential elements of a contract;

(c) conditions which restrict, in an unreasonable way, the contractual freedom of the customer;
(d) conditions which exclude or restrict, in an unreasonable way, legal rights and remedies conferred upon the customer, or provide the supplied remedies he does not legally qualify for;
(e) conditions which impose the burden of proof on the customer, where otherwise the burden of proof would not have been imposed the supplier;
(f) conditions which establish an asymmetrical mechanism of linkage to the index;
(g) conditions which exclude or restrict the customers' right to invoke in court specified facts, or which may cause a deviation from the usual rules of evidence;
(h) conditions which require the customer to confirm or declare that he has read the contract, or is aware of a particular matter.

339. According to section 5(a) a condition which excludes or limits the customer's right of recourse to the court is void.

340. According to section 5(b), a condition, which exclude or restrict, partially or fully, the supplier's liability for bodily harm inflicted on the costumer, or his liability for a malicious act, are void.

E. The System of Control

341. As mentioned above, the Law provides for a combined system of control: judicial control, conducted by the regular courts, and administrative control, conducted by the Tribunal that was established by the law.

342. The court's control is naturally restricted to legal proceedings already taking place between a supplier and a customer. In such proceedings, the court may find, having regard to the terms of the contract in their entirety and to concrete circumstance, that a contractual term is disadvantageous to the customer; in such a case, the court is authorized to annul the term or to alter it to such extent as is necessary to remedy its disadvantageous character.

343. When the court (but not the Tribunal) examines general terms in standard form contracts, it may also resort to the application of all traditional contract doctrines and devices. Thus, the whole corpus of the General Contracts Law co-exists with the provisions of the Standard Contracts Law. Of special interest in this context are those provisions of the General Contracts Law that allow a contracting party to rescind a contract because of misrepresentation (section 15), even if done passively (section 15, second part) or because of economic duress (section 17) or extortion (section 18). The doctrines of good faith and public policy also apply, in principle, to standard terms. However, the provisions of the Standard Contract Law are usually sufficient to solve the problems encountered in most common economic transactions.

344. The Tribunal's control is probably the most important innovation of the Standard Contracts Law. The Law allows the Tribunal to invalidate a standard contract, or a term of the contract. The examination of the general terms in the Tribunal takes place in the abstract, before a specific contract has actually been formed. Section 17 of the Law grants the Tribunal supervisory and enforcement powers that enable it to issue warrants and monitor the compliance to decisions given.

345. In the past, the Tribunal had the authority to approve a standard contract and thus immunize it from judicial intervention. Nevertheless, this authority was revoked in an amendment to the Law legislated in 2014, mostly due to the fact that in practice, few suppliers applied to the Tribunal in order to approve their standard contract.

§3. Conditional Contracts

I. Introduction: Suspensory and Resolutory Conditions

346. Section 27(a) of the General Contracts Law provides as follows:

> A contract may depend on the fulfilment of a condition (hereinafter referred to as a 'suspensory condition') or may cease upon the fulfilment of a condition (hereinafter referred to as a 'resolutory condition').

347. The statutory arrangement governing conditional contracts distinguishes between suspensory and resolutory conditions. A suspensory condition is a condition upon the fulfilment of which the operative consequences and efficacy of the contract are contingent. A resolutory condition is a condition upon the fulfilment of which the contract ceases. In both cases the condition refers to an uncertain event, external to the contract itself. The validity of the operative obligations included in a suspensory conditional contract will remain suspended and imperfect unless and until the condition is fulfilled. By contrast, a resolutory conditional contract ceases to be valid when the condition is fulfilled.

348. The question whether a contract is absolute or conditional, and whether a condition is suspensory or resolutory, will be determined by reference to the intentions of the parties, as revealed either by the contract itself, or by the circumstances of the case.

349. The distinction between the two types of conditions has implications for the rules of evidence: In the case of a suspensory condition the burden is on the party seeking performance of the contract to establish the fulfilment of the condition; in the case of a resolutory condition this burden falls on the party seeking to avoid performance of the contract.

350. Both a suspensory conditional contract and a resolutory conditional contract constitute a complete contract from the moment of the contract's formation. The fulfilment or lack of fulfilment of the condition determines the operative scope of the contract.

II. Presumption Concerning Suspensory Conditions

351. Section 27(b) of the Law provides as follows:

> Where a contract requires the consent of a third party or a licence under any enactment, the receipt of such consent or licence is presumed to be a suspensory condition.

352. Clearly, the presumption in section 27(b) may be rebutted. For example, where the parties have stipulated, or intended, that the receipt of the required licence counts as a contractual obligation to be performed by one of the parties. Failure to receive the licence will, in such cases, amount to a breach of the contract. Reliance on section 27(b) will be unnecessary where the parties have expressly stipulated that receipt of the required third party's consent or licence constitutes a suspensory condition, or where their intentions to this effect can be inferred from the contract or the circumstances of the case.

353. The purpose of section 27(b) is to avoid invalidity on grounds of illegality. Instead of viewing a contract requiring a licence which has yet to be received as illegal, and thus void, the statutory provision attributes to the parties an intention to condition the contract on the receipt of the licence. Hence, the provision of section 27(b) reflects the general principle of contractual interpretation preferring the preservation of the contract's validity to its avoidance.[81]

III. Conditional Contracts: Substantive Aspects

354. Conditional contracts, like unconditional ones, are made by way of offer and acceptance. The contract is complete and binds on the parties from the moment it is made, regardless of whether the condition is suspensory or resolutory.

355. During the intermediary period between the formation of the contract and the fulfilment of the condition, the existence of the contract is conditional. Upon the fulfilment or non-fulfilment of the condition the contract will either become void or an ordinary, unconditional contract.

356. In the case of a suspensory conditional contract, the parties will be bound by the contract during the intermediary period. However, during this period, actions

81. This principle of contractual interpretation has been given statutory expression by the provision of s. 25(b) of the law, discussed above at paras 291–293.

for enforcement or for compensation for non-performance, will not be possible. The contract is 'frozen', and the liabilities and rights of the parties thereunder are contingent on the fulfilment of the condition. Therefore, where a party performs his obligations under the contract during this period, he will be entitled to restitution in accordance with the general principles of unjust enrichment. However, such contingent rights are assignable and constitute part of the entitled party's estate.

357. By contrast, a resolutory conditional contract will be entirely valid and binding during the intermediary period. The rights and obligations under the contract will be unconditional as from the moment of the formation of the contract.

358. Upon the fulfilment of a suspensory condition, the conditional contract becomes an ordinary, unconditional contract.

359. Upon the fulfilment of a resolutory condition, the conditional contract becomes void. The view that such (automatic) avoidance of the contract is prospective only, is supported by the language of section 27(a) which states that the contract 'ceases' upon the fulfilment of the resolutory condition. Pursuant to the general principles of unjust enrichment, and the provisions of section 21 of the law, the avoidance of the contract results in a mutual obligation of restitution.

360. In order to avoid prolonging the uncertainty inherent in the intermediary period between the formation of a conditional contract and the fulfilment of non-fulfilment of the condition, section 29 of the law provides as follows:

> Where a contract is subject to a condition and the condition is not fulfilled within the period fixed therefor or, where no period has been fixed, within a reasonable time after the making of the contract, then, in the case of a suspensory condition, the contract or in the case of a resolutory condition, the condition shall become void.

361. Hence, where the parties to the contract have fixed a period for the fulfilment of the condition, it is this period which will be relevant is assessing the validity of the contract. Where no such period has been fixed, the condition must be fulfilled within reasonable time after the formation of the contract. Reasonableness in this context is subject to change in accordance with developments which occur after the signing of the contract and with the conduct of the parties.[82]

362. Where a suspensory condition is not fulfilled, either within the fixed period or reasonable time, the contract becomes void. In the absence of a contrary contractual provision, such avoidance will be retrospective:[83] the contract will be viewed as not having existed at all, and the parties will be entitled to receive, and obligated to make, restitution.

---

82. *See Shamir v. Hoch* (1983) 37(3) PD 393.
83. *See Hagahna Ltd. v. Namdah Ltd.* (1986) 40(4) PD 369, 370.

363. Where a resolutory condition is not fulfilled within the said periods, the conditional contract becomes unconditional, and the resolutory condition becomes void.

IV. Prevention of the Breach of a Suspensory Conditional Contract

364. Section 27(c) of the law provides as follows:

> Where a contract is subject to a suspensory condition, each party is entitled to relief to prevent its breach even before the condition is fulfilled.

365. The aim of this provision is to protect the conditional contract during the intermediary period after the formation of the contract and before the fulfilment of the suspensory condition. The provision results in a somewhat unusual contract: a contract which cannot be enforced, but one in respect of which an action may be brought in order to prevent its breach. Hence, during the intermediary period, a suspensory conditional contract may be compared to a contract breached by an anticipatory breach: In both cases the injured party will be entitled – even before the obligation to perform the contract comes into effect – to relief so as to prevent the breach of the contract.[84]

V. Frustration of Condition

366. Section 28 of the Law provides as follows:

> (a) Where a contract is subject to a suspensory condition and one party prevents fulfilment of the condition, such party is not entitled to rely on the non-fulfilment.
> (b) Where a contract is subject to a resolutory condition and one party causes fulfilment of such condition, such party is not entitled to rely on such fulfilment.
> (c) The provisions of this section shall not apply where the condition is something that according to the contract a party is at liberty to do or not to do or where a party does not prevent or cause the fulfilment of the condition wilfully or negligently.

367. The frustration provided for in section 28 differs from frustration of a contract.[85] Frustration of a condition is a wilful intervention of a party to the contract, aimed at either preventing the fulfilment of a suspensory condition, or causing the fulfilment of a resolutory condition. In both cases of frustration of a condition, the party will be in breach of the obligation to act in accordance with the spirit of the contract.

---

84. For further discussion of anticipatory breach, *see* paras 460–464.
85. For discussion of frustration of contracts, *see* paras 401–443.

368. Section 28 expresses the validity of the contract during the intermediary stage – from the formation of the conditional contract until the occurrence of the condition. Like section 27(c) discussed above, the provisions of section 28 originate from the principle of good faith. The section imposes a fiduciary duty upon the parties and requires them to act in good faith.

369. Subsections 28(a) and 28(b) create a kind of a statutory estoppel: A party who prevents the fulfilment of a suspensory condition will be estopped from relying on the non-fulfilment; a party who causes the fulfilment of a resolutory condition will be estopped from relying on such fulfilment.

370. Section 28(c), however, creates two alternative defence claims that can be raised by the party seeking to rely on either the non-fulfilment of a suspensory condition, or the fulfilment of a resolutory condition, despite the fact that they were caused by him.

371. The first defence claim materializes when the party acted within the scope of rights and liberties conveyed upon him by the contract. This defence derives from the principle of freedom of contract and the priority given to the intention of the parties.

372. The second defence claim materializes when the party that prevented the fulfilment of a suspensory condition or caused the fulfilment of a resolutory condition acted wilfully (a subjective test) or negligently (an objective test).

Chapter 4. Privity of Contract

§1. Contract for the Benefit of a Third Party

373. One of the major innovations of the General Contracts Law is the recognition of the concept of a contract for the benefit of a third person, in Chapter 4 of the Law. Since the enactment of the General Contracts Law, Israeli law expressly recognizes the contractual right of a third-party beneficiary.

374. Chapter 4 is based on the principles of the autonomy of the will and the freedom of contract. The contracting parties' power to confer a right upon a person, who is not a party to the contract, and the recognition of such a right, derive from these principles.

375. The innovation of Chapter 4 lies in the recognition of the right of the third party to demand the fulfilment of the contract. According to its sources and attributes, this right is a contractual right. It originates from the contract, as an outcome of offer and acceptance of the parties to the contract. The same contract that defines the scope and contents of the third-party beneficiary's right and governs its effect, also creates the correlative duty of the promisor.

376. The contracting parties' will in a contract for the benefit of a third party receives practical expression in two stages: the first is the formation of the contract, the second is the notice given to the third party of his right. Accordingly, in the first stage the third party's right is conferred and in the second stage it becomes irrevocable. In each stage the parties have to express their will. Even more so: regarding the parties' will as the dominant factor in creating the third party's right and in making such right irrevocable, indicates that the provisions of Chapter 4 are *ius dispositivum*, i.e., the parties may contract out of these provisions by expressing a contrary intention.

377. Section 34 of the Law grants the third-party beneficiary 'the right to demand fulfilment of' an obligation in a contract. In order for such right to be conferred, section 34 requires that the parties' intention to confer that right on the third party should be 'apparent from the contract'. The intention may therefore be expressly stated in the contract, or implied from the intention of the parties.

378. The right of the third party is conferred only upon the direct beneficiary, not upon an incidental one. An incidental beneficiary is a person who is affected by the contract and may benefit from its performance, but cannot demand this performance in law. The parties determine whether a beneficiary is a direct beneficiary or an incidental beneficiary, by determining whether to confer upon him an enforceable right.

379. Section 36 provides that the right of the third party cannot be altered or terminated after one of the parties has given a notice to the beneficiary of his right. So long as neither of the parties has informed the beneficiary of his right under the contract, the parties may modify or terminate the beneficiary's right by altering the contract.

380. Irrevocability of a third-party beneficiary's right is thus neither a condition nor a consequence of the recognition of this right. Whether it is revocable or irrevocable depends solely on the parties' declarations of will. The revocability of the right is an outcome of its contractual nature and source. As parties create it by their own volition, they can also revoke it by mutual consent.

381. Thus, the third party's right is created by the contract in his favour and it becomes irrevocable once one of the parties informs the beneficiary of his right. In the interval between the formation of the contract in favour of a third party and the notice given to the beneficiary of his right, the beneficiary has a complete, enforceable right, although a fragile right which is subject to the contracting parties' power to vary or terminate it.

382. Section 35 provides that the third party may reject his right to demand fulfilment of the contract. He may do this by informing one of the parties to the contract of his rejection. Such rejection has a retroactive effect and must take place within reasonable time after one of the parties informs the beneficiary of his right.

383. As section 37 provides the right of the third-party beneficiary does not extend beyond its contractual source. It is, therefore, subject to any plea arising from the contract and 'available to the debtor against the creditor in connection with the obligation'.

§2. Transfer of Contractual Rights

384. The transfer of contractual rights is governed in Israel by the Transfer of Obligations Law, 1969. The transferred right can be a conditional right or a future right. The transfer of the contractual right takes effect right away, and the right is transferred to the transferee. No further action is necessary, as the right becomes the transferee's property. An important characteristic of the transfer of contractual rights is that the debtor's consent is not required for such a transfer to take effect. The right is transferred to the transferee as it is, and no new legal relations are established. The transfer may relate to the whole or part of the right, and may be conditional or by way of a charge.

385. The Law does not establish a special form of transfer; rather, the form depends on the type of the right being transferred. The relationship between the transferor and the transferee is not dealt with by the Law. This relationship is determined by the contract between the transferor and the transferee, which need not be in writing. The transfer of a contractual right can thus be executed by an oral agreement.

386. A right is transferable only when the identity of the creditor is of no importance to the debtor. It seems, therefore, that a right for the services of an employee, or a right accruing from an insurance contract, is non-transferrable (unless the debtor agrees to the transfer).

387. The right to transfer can be restricted in a contract between the debtor and the creditor. The consequences of a transfer which takes place in spite of a restricting agreement between the debtor and the creditor amounts to a breach of contract, authorizing the debtor to sue for remedies upon breach. The appropriate remedy will be enforcement, enabling the debtor to disregard the transfer and continue considering the transferor as his creditor.

388. Where a transfer of rights is made in breach of an agreement between the creditor and a debtor, the transaction has no effect, and, as a result, the transferee has no right against the debtor. This is true even if the transferee has no knowledge of the agreement. Restrictions on transferability of contractual rights should be narrowly interpreted, in order to protect the bona fide transferee.

389. The transfer of a contractual right results in an immediate change of ownership of the right. Consequently, the old creditor is replaced by the new creditor.

390. The transfer of a right does not alter the right itself nor its terms: the right is transferred as is. All the contractual pleas that were available to the debtor against the creditor-transferor, will be at his disposal against the transferee. Pleas not based on the contract will also be available to the debtor, if they existed at the time that the debtor was notified of the transfer.

391. The debtor may waive the pleas that he has or will have in the future, by a direct promise to the transferee, or in the agreement with the transferor, which will then be considered as a contract in favour of a third party.

392. The law protects the debtor from becoming exposed to a double obligation: if the debtor settles the claim with the transferor prior to being notified of the transfer, or before a written instrument of transfer is delivered to him, he is discharged unless he did not act in good faith. The settlement of the claim discharges the debtor even though the right was transferred. The same rule applies if the debtor settles the claim with the transferee after he was notified, even if the right was not transferred to the transferee, unless he did not act in good faith.

393. As in the case of 'market overt' in the Sale Law, the right of the first transferee takes precedence over the rights of other transferees. However, the transferor does not lose the power to transfer. Thus, if he transferred to a second transferee, and he notified the debtor of the second transfer before notifying him of the first one, the second transferee becomes the owner of the right.

394. A liability may be transferred by an agreement between the debtor and the transferee to whom the creditor has given his consent, unless its transferability is negated or restricted by law. The debtor is discharged and a direct relationship is established between the creditor and the transferee. Unlike the transfer of a right, which does not require the debtor's consent, the transfer of liability requires the creditor's consent. However, such consent need not be explicit, and may be inferred from the creditor's conduct. An agreement between the debtor and the transferee is necessary. Yet, mere agreement between the transferee and creditor will not suffice, since the debtor may be interested in personally fulfilling his liability.

395. The transfer of liability does not alter the right nor its terms. As in the transfer of rights, the debtor's pleas are preserved: All the pleas available to the debtor against the creditor at the time of transfer shall be available to the transferee.

Chapter 5. Termination of the Contract

§1. Performance and Breach

396. Section 1(a) of the Remedies Law defines the term 'breach' as 'an act or omission in contravention of a contract'.

397. The above definition lays forth a number of leading principles; a breach (an act or an omission) is manifested via behaviour. An undesirable situation will not suffice a party's right to claim damages. The behaviour does not have to entirely prevent the performance of the contract. Behaviour which resulted in the breach of a single obligation is also considered a breach of contract. The definition is broad and includes defective performance, non-performance, refusal to perform and delay in performance. The breach does not necessarily have to be established by an active behaviour, and may be an omission to act. Even non-performance caused by circumstances giving rise to a successful plea of frustration falls within the purview of the definition.

398. However, when the breach is negligible, the court may apply the broad principle of good faith in order to bar a claim by the 'injured party' – defined in section 1(a) as 'a person entitled to performance of a contract which has been broken'. In addition, the Remedies Law itself includes certain provisions – such as those contained in sections 3(4) and 7(b) employing the term 'justice' – which may assist a defendant faced with a claim based on a negligible breach.

399. Most importantly, the definition clarifies that a breach is the behaviour contrary to the contract, i.e., to the consent of the parties as expressed in the contract between them. In accordance to the *Aprofim* ruling[86] the consent of the parties will be interpreted not only according to their explicit agreement, but also according to an agreement inferred from the behaviour of the parties or from the circumstances of the contract's conclusion.

400. The principle adopted by the Remedies Law is that – subject to the principle of good faith – a breach requires no particular mental element. Hence, contractual liability under Israeli law is, in fact, strict: any act or omission in contravention of a contract constitutes a breach, regardless of the intention of the party in breach. A party may desire and actively strive to perform the contract, but if it fails the party will be deemed to have breached the contract. By contrast, a party may relate to the contract with contempt and apathy, and yet not be in breach thereof. The test applied in determining whether the contract has been breached is objective and neutral: The contract and the actual performance are compared and contrasted, and any deviation of the latter from the former will constitute a breach. Even a party who, believing that he is entitled to rescind, gives notice of rescission, may later discover that he has inadvertently breached the contract. However, this

86. Discussed above at paras 283 et seq.

strict approach may be mitigated both by the principle of good faith and by certain provisions based on justice incorporated into the Remedies Law itself.[87]

§2. Impossibility, Frustration and Hardship: 'The Unforeseen'

I. Exemption by Reason of Frustration of the Contract

A. *Frustration*

401. Section 18(a) of the Remedies Law provides as follows:

> Where the breach of contract is the result of circumstances which at the time of making the contract the person in breach did not know of or foresee and need not have known of or foreseen, and which he could not have avoided, and performance of the contract under these circumstances is impossible or fundamentally different from what was agreed between the parties, the breach shall not give cause for enforcement of the contract or for compensation.

402. It follows from the above section that a frustrating event, preventing performance of the contract, does not negate the existence of a breach: the contract is breached even if non-performance results from frustration. This apparent anomaly can be explained by the width and neutrality of the definition of 'breach' in section 1: 'an act or omission in contravention of a contact'.

403. Section 18(a) stipulates three conditions each of which must be satisfied before the party in breach will be exempt from the ordinary consequences of breach:

(1) lack of knowledge or foresight – actual or potential – of the frustrating circumstances;
(2) inability to avoid such circumstances; and
(3) occurrence of circumstances frustrating performance of the contract.

The burden of proof lies on the party claiming frustration – usually the party in breach – who must show that all three conditions are met.

B. *The Foreseeability Test*

404. With regard to the first of these three necessary conditions, section 18(a) of the Remedies Law requires the application of both a subjective and objective test: The actual knowledge or foresight of the party in breach must be examined, as well as his knowledge or foresight according to the standard provided by the 'reasonable person'. Hence, the first condition will not be satisfied where the party in breach had

87. For further discussion, *see* para. 459.

either actual or potential knowledge or foresight of the frustrating circumstances. It must be shown by the party on whom the burden of proof lies, that at the time of formation the contract, none of these four possible alternatives existed.

405. In applying the objective test, the court will examine whether the reasonable person, placed in the position of the party in breach, and bearing in mind the logic and circumstances of the actual transaction, should have known of or foreseen the frustrating event. Unforeseeability in this context has been construed narrowly by the courts; hence, in several cases it has been ruled that natural calamities such as frost or rain were reasonably foreseeable.[88] Dicta even exist to the effect that, given the realities of life in Israel, the outbreak of war is reasonably foreseeable and thus does not constitute a frustrating event.[89] In other cases it has been ruled that certain acts or omissions of third parties, such as the refusal to vacate land, were not unforeseeable. In short, the tendency evinced by case law was to treat the party in breach as one who should have foreseen common frustrating events, in addition to those that were possible to foresee. The narrow interpretation of the element of foreseeability, reflected the general approach of the courts towards the plea of frustration. This approach had, in fact, resulted in section 18(a) of the Remedies Law remaining a 'dead letter'.

406. This rigid approach is incompatible with liberal modern trends. Indeed, the Supreme Court ruled that the test of foreseeability must be applied to the practical implications of the unforeseeable event, and not to the actual event.[90]

C. The Risk Test

407. Covid-19 pandemic in 2020, the shutdown and the quarantine in its wake, caused, in Israel as all over the world, legal problems. In the area of contract law these problems revolved around the themes of 'force majeure', 'act of state' and 'frustration'. The inability of many contracting parties to perform their contractual obligations due to the financial and economic crisis, made clear that a new approach to frustration is required. This new situation caused the Israeli legal community to re-evaluate the Civil Code Bill and mainly the solution provided by the codification committee aimed at regulating situations of frustration.[91] The main recommendation in the chapter on frustration in the bill was to replace the foreseeability test with a new and modern test, the risk test.

408. The risk test originates from the American legal system, where sections within the Restatement and within the U.C.C. determine that a party will not be able to claim frustration in cases where he had undertaken a risk.

---

88. *See*, e.g., *Shagan v. Madar* (1974) PD 29(1) 445; *Kfar Chassidim v. Abraham* (1985) 39(2) PD 490.
89. *Katz v. Nitzchoni Mizrachi* (1979) 33(3) PD 639, 643 (per Landau J.).
90. *Regev v. Ministry of Defence* (2000) 54(5) PD 517 (per Englard J.).
91. The codification efforts are discussed above at para. 20.

409. Section 131(a) of the forthcoming Civil Code applies the risk test to Israeli law and provides: 'When a frustrating event occurs, and the risk of such an event and its outcome is not imposed on the party whose obligations were frustrated, the contract shall expire on the occurrence of the frustrating event.'

410. The claim for frustration will therefore be subject to the risk test, by which the results of the frustrating event are not imposed on the party whose obligations or rights had been frustrated. A prerequisite for the acceptance of a claim of frustration is that the party claiming frustration of the contract had undertaken the risk of the occurrence of the event upon himself. Failure to undertake risk will be a prerequisite to frustration.

411. A risk may be undertaken either expressly or implied from circumstances or behaviour. Section 131(b) of the Civil Code provides: 'A party to the contract shall be considered as having undertaken a risk as aforesaid in section (a), if he undertook the risk upon himself either explicitly or implicitly, or if it were just to impose the aforesaid risk upon him'.

412. Thus, the undertaking of a risk involving the occurrence of a certain event may be assumed either expressly by the party, as a stipulation in the contract, or implied by circumstances at the time of the conclusion of the contract, commercial practice, and characteristics of the parties.

413. In the event where the contract or its circumstances fail to indicate which party will assume responsibility for the risk of an extreme change in circumstances, the suffix of the section 131(b) provides that it shall be decided according to what the court deems just. Such justice considerations are based on the economic analysis of contract law, examining which party could have insured itself and prevented the damage at the lowest cost.

414. According to the principle of freedom of contract, and the consequential rule pertaining to the upholding of agreements, when the risk was neither expressly nor implicitly undertaken by one of the parties, the creditor's interest should be preferred over that of the debtor. In the normal state of affairs, the debtor is to be responsible for insuring himself against the unexpected turn of events.

D. Inability to Avoid Frustration

415. The second condition of frustration, under section 18(a) of the Remedies Law, is that the party in breach of the contract 'could not have avoided' the frustrating circumstances. This condition relates to the actual person in breach and not to the reasonable person. It is sufficient to show that the former could not have avoided the frustrating circumstances. It follows from this condition that self-induced frustration will not amount to frustration subject to section 18(a): actions performed by the party in breach could have been avoided.

416. With the enactment of the forthcoming Civil Code, this condition will be concluded from the rationale of the above-mentioned risk test and from the principle of good faith.

E. Frustrating Circumstances

417. The third condition of frustration, under section 18(a) of the Remedies Law, is that 'the performance of the contract is impossible or fundamentally different from what was agreed between the parties'.

1. Impossibility

418. The first category of frustrating circumstances, which is based on impossibility, may itself be broken down into four sub-categories: disappearance of the subject of the contract; injury to the means or device intended to perform the contract; death or incapacity of the party in breach; legal impossibility.

419. The first of these refers to circumstances in which, as a result of force majeure, such as fire, earthquake or flood, the contract cannot be performed.

420. The second sub-category refers to circumstances in which the means intended to carry out the contract were destroyed, (a sunken ship or stolen means of transportation). However, when the contract may be implemented using other measures, a claim for frustration will be rejected.

421. The third sub-category will apply only in those cases where it can be shown that upon its proper construction, performance of the contract entailed the rendering of personal services by the party in breach.

422. The fourth sub-category requires that a distinction be drawn between illegality which was inherent in the contract– governed by the provisions of section 30 of the General Contracts Law – and illegality which is subsequent to the formation of the contract – governed by section 18(a) of the Remedies Law.

2. Common Mistake

423. A distinction must be made between frustrating events which occurred prior to the contract's formation and frustrating circumstances occurring after its formation. An additional sub-category, namely that of common mistake, is problematic. Since section 18(a) does not explicitly indicate the time of the occurrence of the frustrating circumstances, a literal interpretation of the section can support the conclusion that the section also applies to situations where the frustrating event took place prior to the formation of the contract. Traditionally however such situations have been treated by the common law not as instances of frustration but rather as falling within the ambit of the doctrine of mistake (section 14 of the General Contracts Law).[92] The language of section 18(a), concerning the inability of the party in breach to avoid the frustrating circumstances, supports this view. The condition of inability to avoid the frustrating circumstances appears to foresee the future and to apply only with regard to events taking place after the contact was made.

424. Section 130 of the forthcoming Civil Code also clarifies that a frustrating event is only an event which occurred after the conclusion of the contract.

3. Fundamental Difference

425. Within the scope of frustrating circumstances referred to in section 18 are those circumstances which do not necessarily cause the performance of the contract to be impossible, but rather result in the performance of the contract to be fundamentally different from that which was agreed upon between the parties. A comparison must be made, in retrospect, between the performance of the contract in view of the new circumstances in question, and the original contractual agreement between the parties. Where a significant, 'fundamental', difference is found to exist between the two, the contract will be deemed frustrated (assuming the other necessary conditions for frustration are met as well). The difference, however, must be extreme and far-reaching.

4. Impracticability

426. The 'fundamental difference' test is sufficiently broad and flexible to encompass two doctrines which have developed within the framework of Anglo-American law relating to frustration. The first of these, based on the notion of impracticability, allows for frustration in cases where performance of the contract is not practicable in view of the high cost of performance, provided such cost was due to unforeseeable events which altered the substance of the contract performance. Although the doctrine of impracticability has yet to be applied by the courts, dicta exists to the effect that, in appropriate circumstances, the doctrine might even be applicable to situations where the impracticability does not necessarily stem from the high cost of performance.[93]

5. Frustration of the Purpose

427. The second of the two doctrines applies to situations where the purpose of the contract has been frustrated as a result of the occurrence of external events over

92. Discussed above at paras 185–200.
93. *Natan v. Strode* (1988) 42(1) PD 661, 675 (per Elon J.).

which the parties had no control.[94] As in the case of the doctrine of impracticability, the doctrine based on frustration of the contract's purpose has yet to be applied. However, the breadth of section 18, together with the general application of the basic principle of good faith, supports the view that this doctrine too is embraced by the provision of section 18 relating to a fundamental change.

428. Indeed, section 130 of the forthcoming Civil Code includes the frustration of the purpose within the definition of a frustrating event.

6. Anticipatory Frustration

429. Where it is apparent from the circumstances of the case, even before the time for performance of the contract has arrived, that such performance will be impossible or fundamentally different from which was agreed upon, then, provided the other necessary conditions of frustration are also complied, the party, injured by the anticipated frustration, is entitled to rescind the contract immediately and to refrain from performance of its own obligations thereunder. In such circumstances the party will not be entitled to enforcement or to compensation. This approach involves a combined application of the doctrine of frustration and the doctrine of anticipatory breach provided in section 17 of the Remedies Law.[95]

F. Contracting Out

430. The laws of frustration are dispositive and are subject to the stipulations of the parties to the contract, who may choose a different result than the one provided by section 18. While such stipulations may simply define certain frustrating events as known or foreseen by the parties, thereby negating one of the necessary conditions of frustration, these stipulations may also create absolute contractual liability, regardless of whatever subsequent circumstances or events occur, foreseen or otherwise.

431. According to the new risk test within the forthcoming Civil Code, the party which undertook the risk is to assume responsibility, thus giving precedence to the stipulations of the parties between themselves.

II. Consequences of Frustration

A. Effect of Frustration

432. Section 2 of the Remedies Law provides as follows:

---

94. The source of this doctrine is the famous series of the 'coronation cases'. *See, e.g.*, *Krell v. Henry* [1903] 2 KB 740.
95. For further discussion regarding s. 17 of the Remedies Law, *see* paras 460–464.

> Where a contract has been breached, the injured party is entitled to claim its enforcement or to rescind the contract, and in addition to or in lieu of one of the said remedies he is entitled to compensation, all as provided in this law.

433. However, pursuant to section 18(a), where the contract has been breached in circumstances giving rise to a successful plea of frustration, the injured party will not be entitled to an enforcement or compensation. The injured party will be still entitled to rescind the contract. Moreover, in contrast to the approach taken by English Law, according to which frustration automatically results in the termination of the contract, under Israeli law, the frustrated contract will remain valid and binding unless and until it is rescinded by the injured party.[96]

434. In contrast to the current legal position, the forthcoming Civil Code adopts the English approach, stating in section 131(a) that a frustrating event will provide grounds for the termination of the contract upon the moment of frustration and thereon.

B. Remedies

435. Section 18(b) of the Remedies Law provides:

> In the cases referred to in subsection (a), the Court may, whether or not the contract has been rescinded, require each party to restore to the other party what he has received under the contract or, at his choice as provided in section 9, to pay him the value thereof, and require the person in breach to indemnify the injured party for expenses reasonably incurred and liabilities reasonably contracted by him for the performance of the contract, all if and in so far as the Court deems it just to do so in the circumstances of the case.

436. In contrast to the general rule stipulated in section 9, rescission of a frustrated contract will not automatically result in a right to restitution. In the context of frustration, restitution is subject to the court's discretion. It is not, however, contingent on rescission.

437. The purpose of the reference in section 18(b) to section 9 is, presumably, to grant the injured party, in the context of frustration, the same preference over the party in breach, as that which is granted to it under section 9. In other words, by virtue of the reference to section 9, where the court, pursuant to section 18(b), requires each party to restore to the other party what it has received under the contract, the injured party may choose instead to pay or be paid the value thereof.

438. The power of the court to require restitution where a contract has been frustrated is aimed at balancing between the respective interests of the parties, and distributing the damage among them in a just and rational manner. The court is to

96. *Shamir v. Hoch* (1983) 37(3) PD 393, 414.

exercise its discretion in this context subject to the requirements of justice in the circumstances of the case. Hence, the court's discretion is broad and flexible.

C. Remedies: Indemnity

439. In contrast to the position concerning restitution, the discretion of the court concerning indemnity can be exercised only in favour of the injured party. The purpose of section 18(b) is to place the injured party as close as possible to the position it was in at the eve of entering the contract. The obligation of the party in breach extends to expenses incurred and liabilities contracted by the injured party for the performance of the contract, provided such expenses and liabilities were reasonable. The provision affords protection to the reliance interest of the injured party who acted reasonably in the belief that the contract would be performed.

D. Contracting Out

440. While the parties to a contract cannot derogate from the power granted to the courts under section 18(b), the courts will most certainly take into account and strive to give effect to stipulations in the contract which purport to contract out of the mutual right of restitution, or of the injured party's right of indemnity.

E. In the Civil Code

441. With the enactment of the forthcoming Civil Code, the obligation of restitution and the right of indemnification will create effective judicial tools to enable a balanced distribution of damage between the parties. These provisions reflect modern trends of solidarity, equality, good faith and justice.

442. The obligation of restitution was established in the forthcoming Civil Code, by virtue of unjust enrichment, alongside judicial discretion empowered to exempt a party from restitution contingent on considerations of justice

443. The forthcoming Civil Code also empowers the court with discretion to indemnify each of the parties for reasonable expenses incurred and for reasonable commitments he may have made for the performance of the contract.

Chapter 6. Remedies

§1. General Provisions

444. Section 2 of the Remedies Law provides as follows:

> Where a contract has been broken, the injured party is entitled to claim its enforcement or to rescind the contract, and in addition to or in lieu of one of the said remedies he is entitled to compensation, all as provided in this law.[97]

445. It follows from the above provision that a breach is a condition precedent of a remedy: the remedies referred to in section 2 are made available by the law to the injured party only after there has been a breach of the contract.

446. A further condition precedent of a remedy is the contract itself: No remedy will be available unless there is an existing and valid contract. Hence, where the contract is invalid for any reason whatsoever it cannot be breached and consequently no remedy will be available.

447. A breach entitles the injured party to a remedy, namely, enforcement, rescission and compensation. A breach, even a fundamental one, will not in itself annul the contract. Instead, the breach will entitle the injured party to choose between rescission of the contract or a claim for its enforcement. Where the injured party chooses not to rescind the contract, the contract remains valid and binding despite the breach.

448. Section 2 lists the principal remedies and determines the relation between them. The first two remedies, rescission and enforcement, are mutually exclusive: in view of their opposing nature, the injured party cannot both rescind and be granted an order of enforcement. Instead, he must choose between them. While enforcement is based on a court order instructing the party in breach to perform the contract, rescission annuls the contractual obligations not yet performed, and puts the injured party in the same position he was in before making the contract (*restitution in integrum*). By contrast, in appropriate circumstances a claim for compensation may be made, either in conjunction with a claim for enforcement, in addition to rescission or independently of both these remedies. Moreover, in circumstances where the conditions of rescission and enforcement are not satisfied, the injured party will have no choice but to settle for a claim for compensation.

449. The Remedies Law is divided into three chapters. The first chapter contains only two sections, the first of which provides a set of definitions to some basic terms, such as beach, damages and the remedy of enforcement. Section 2 presents the remedies available and clarifies the interrelations between them. The second

---

97. For further discussion regarding the topics covered in this chapter, *see* Gabriela Shalev & Yehuda Adar, *The Law of Remedies in a Mixed Jurisdiction: The Israeli Experience*, 23 Tulane European Civil Law Forum 111 (2008).

chapter elaborates on each of the three remedies mentioned in section 2. Sections 3 to 5 entitle the injured party a right to enforcement while defining the limit to this right. Sections 6 to 9 stipulate provisions for terminations including the parties' right to restitution. Sections 10 to 16 determine the injured party's right to compensatory damages, including liquidated damages, the amount of which may be reduced by the court if greatly disproportionate to the damage reasonably foreseeable as a result of the breach at the time of formation. Finally, the third chapter, sections 17 to 20, includes several important issues, such as anticipatory breach, frustration of the contract and the self-help remedies of detention (lien) and set-off. The last five sections concern matters of jurisdiction and procedure. The exercise of the injured party's rights regarding all three of the main remedies is subject to the principle of good faith under section 39 of the Remedies Law.

§2. Contractual Liability: Strict Liability?

I. The Basic Rule

450. The basic approach in contract law in Israel (as opposed to penal law and a great part of tort law) is that of strict liability. The test of a breach of contract is an objective and neutral one; any diversion from the contract constitutes a breach, regardless of the party's justified explanation. Liability exists as long as an obligation in the contract has not been performed, regardless of the degree of moral blame either on the debtor's part or due to the creditors conduct. This assumption is firmly established in rulings of the Supreme Court.[98] A breach of contract may transpire despite best endeavours and desire of a party to perform the contract, so long as he does not actually fulfil his contractual obligation. There is also no requirement for the awareness of the breaching party regarding the breach. It does not matter whether he was aware that his actions caused the breach in contract or not.

II. Exceptions to the Rule

451. Despite the basic approach of strict liability, some legal rules and principles mitigate this approach and serve to infuse flexibility and social values into contract law. These rules are discussed below.

A. Best Endeavours Obligation

452. In some cases, contractual liability will be interpreted as a liability to use best endeavours and not necessarily to achieve a specific result. The distinction between an obligation to use best endeavours (*obligations de moyens)* and an obligation to produce a particular result (*Obligations de résultat)* originates from the

98. *Eximin v. Textile and Footwear* (1993) 47(4) PD 64, 81. Available in English at http://cisgw3.law.pace.edu/cases/930822i5.html.

French legal system. In most common contracts, like sale or lease contracts, the primary obligation is to produce a result. However, professionals, like doctors or lawyers, usually do not commit to a specific result, but rather to administer their best reasonable endeavours. Contractual interpretation will be applied in order to discern whether the obligation is to achieve a result or only to use best endeavour.

B. Suspension of Perfomance (Exceptio Non Adimpleti Contractus)

453. Section 43(a) of the General Contracts Law deals with suspension of performance (*exceptio non adimpleti contractus*) and provides as follows:

(a) The date for the fulfilment of the obligation is postponed –

(1) if its fulfilment at the due date is prevented by a circumstance depending on the creditor – until the obstacle has been removed;
(2) if its fulfilment is conditional upon the prior fulfilment of an obligation by the creditor, until that obligation has been fulfilled.
(3) If the parties must fulfil their obligations pari passu – so long as the creditor is not prepared to fulfil the obligation imposed on him.

454. Section 43(a)(1) of the General Contracts Law addresses the situation where the creditor is responsible for preventing the obligor's fulfilment of the obligation. In this situation the debtor does not have to fulfil his obligation until the obstacle has been removed.

455. The claim that an act or omission is not 'in contravention of a contract' and does not constitute a breach, because the other party has not yet fulfilled his obligation, may also be raised where the creditor has not yet fulfilled his obligation (section 43(a)(2)) or where the parties' obligations are concurrent (section 43(a)(3)).

456. Concurrent obligations are parallel obligations of the parties to a mutual contract which must be fulfilled *pari passu*, i.e., obligations which must be fulfilled at one and the same time. In a contract in which the obligations are concurrent, a connection exists between the respective performances of each party's obligation. Section 43(a)(3) clarifies that in such cases the date for the fulfilment of an obligation is postponed so long as the creditor is not prepared to fulfil the obligation imposed on him. In other words, the moment one of the parties is not prepared to fulfil his obligation, the date for fulfilment of the other party's obligation is postponed. However, preparedness (i.e., willingness and ability) on the part of one party to fulfil his obligation will suffice to convert non-performance by the other party into a breach.[99]

99. *Jerby v. Heighblum* (1976) 30(2) PD 673.

457. Case law has treated the question of whether or not contractual obligations are concurrent as a matter of contractual interpretation, namely a matter of determining the intention of the parties.[100]

C. *'De Minimis'*

458. According to the *de minimis* principle in penal and tort law, there is no justification for legal action when the injury to the plaintiff is marginal and insignificant. However, this principle was not incorporated within contract law. The Remedies Law treats a slight breach as a significant one, and all kinds of breach entitle the injured party to remedies. Nonetheless, the principle of good faith empowers the court to employ this principle in order to reject a claim pertaining to a minor breach which evoked insignificant repercussions.[101]

D. *Good Faith and Contract Interpretation*

459. Finally, the principle of good faith and the rules of contract interpretation are most important in shaping the Israeli contract law and in mitigating the rule of contractual strict liability.[102]

§3. ANTICIPATORY BREACH

460. Section 17 of the Remedies Law establishes the Common Law doctrine of anticipatory breach within Israeli contract law,[103] and provides as follows:

> Where a party to the contract indicates his intention not to perform it or where it appears from the circumstances that he will be unable or unwilling to perform it, the other party is entitled to the remedies under this law even before the time set for the performance of the contract; however, in making an enforcement order the court shall not direct that an obligation shall be carried out before the time set for its performance.

461. An anticipatory breach of the contract occurs before the time set for the performance of the contract. Section 17 mentions two alternatives or two classes of cases in which the injured party is entitled to contractual remedies before the time for performance has arrived. The first alternative, where the other party indicates his intention not to perform the contract; the second alternative, where it appears from the circumstances that the party will be unable to perform the contract.

---

100. *Adoram v. Achim Bchor* (1987) 41(1) PD 829, 833.
101. *Jerby v. Ben David* (1991) 45(5) PD 661.
102. Discussed above at para. 287.
103. *See* G. Shalev, *Remedies on Anticipatory Repudiation*, 8 Isr. L. Rev. 123 (1973).

462. Upon the occurrence of an anticipatory breach, the injured party is entitled to the remedies under the Remedies Law, as if the breach had occurred already. The contract is regarded as breached, backdating the performance of the contract and the right to any remedy to the date of the anticipatory breach.

463. The first alternative of anticipatory breach is a subjective one, sometimes referred to as repudiation or renunciation.[104] It occurs when the party in breach indicates his intention not to perform the contract or when circumstances show that he is unwilling to perform it.

464. The second alternative of anticipatory breach is an objective one, sometimes referred to as disablement from performance.[105] It pertains to a situation where it is apparent that the other party will be unable to perform the contract.

§4. Enforcement

I. The Right of Enforcement

465. The right of enforcement is both established and qualified by the provisions of section 3 of the Remedies Law, which provides as follows:

> The injured party is entitled to enforcement of the contract unless one of the following obtains:
>
> (1) The contract is impossible of performance;
> (2) Enforcement of the contract consists in compelling the doing or acceptance of personal work or a personal service;
> (3) Implementation of the enforcement order requires an unreasonable amount of supervision on behalf of a court or an execution office;
> (4) Enforcement of the contract in the circumstances of the case is unjust.

466. The remedy of enforcement is the first and principal remedy afforded under Israeli law in cases of a breach of contract. The right of enforcement arises immediately upon the breach of the contract. Exercising the right requires a court order, and in this sense the remedy of enforcement is different from that of rescission: the right to rescind a contract may be exercised by the injured party automatically.

467. In contrast to the traditional approach of English law, Israeli contract law regards the remedy of enforcement as the major remedy for breach of contract. According to the approach adopted in Chapter 1 of the General Contracts Law, the contract is viewed as founded upon agreement, and as a legal device for realizing the will of the parties; an approach which supports the primacy of the remedy of

104. *See* Guenter H. Treitel, *The Law of Contract* 754 (8th ed. 1991); Allan E. Farnsworth, *Farnsworth on Contracts*, Vol. II, 559–564 (3rd ed. 2004).
105. *Ibid.*

enforcement. The main objective of making a contract is its performance.; hence, the party in breach is under an obligation to perform his original undertaking, and the injured party is entitled to performance of that which was promised to him under the contract.

468. The approach adopted by the Israeli legislator concerning enforcement is also indicative of a social attitude concerning the contractual relation and the importance of keeping contractual promises. Furthermore, in keeping with modern trends, the primacy of the enforcement remedy serves to protect the reasonable expectations and interests of the parties. Finally, requirements of commercial fairness and good faith in business relations support the enforcement remedy, which is closer to the contract and its contents than any other remedy.

II. Means of Enforcement

469. Section 1(a) of the Remedies Law defines the term 'enforcement' as 'enforcement by an order for the discharge of a monetary obligation or some other mandatory order or by a restraining order, and includes enforcement by an order for the repair or removal of the consequences of the breach'. This definition does not describe enforcement itself, but rather the different means of enforcement.

470. In view of the first of the several orders listed above, which is but a particular instance of a mandatory order, monetary obligations, such as the payment of a purchase price or rent, are enforceable. Despite their external similarities, an enforcement order in respect of a monetary obligation is to be distinguished from the remedy of compensation. While a monetary obligation is subject to the exceptions listed in section 3 of the Remedies Law, but not to the obligation concerning mitigation of damages (section 14 of the Remedies Law), the remedy of compensation is subject to the mitigation obligation, but not to the exception in section 3(4), based on justice.

III. Qualifications Concerning Enforcement

471. Section 3 of the Remedies Law lists four exceptions to the general right of enforcement. It provides as follows:

> The injured party is entitled to enforcement of the contract unless one of the following obtains:
>
> (1) the contract is impossible of performance;
> (2) enforcement of the contract consists in compelling the doing or acceptance of personal work or a personal service;
> (3) implementation of the enforcement order requires an unreasonable amount of supervision on behalf of a court or an execution office;
> (4) enforcement of the contract in the circumstances of the case is unjust.

472. The burden of proof of all these exceptions lies on the party in breach, who, in defending himself against an action for enforcement, must establish the elements of the exception in question in order to prove that the injured party is not entitled to enforcement. Success in lifting this burden of proof will not affect the injured party's rights concerning rescission and compensation.

473. A clear example of the first exception, i.e., impossibility of performance, is demonstrated in cases where the object of the contract has been destroyed. Less extreme circumstances, such as the transfer of the object of the contract – with or without the knowledge of the party in breach – to a third party, will also suffice to establish the exception. However, the party in breach must show that performance is entirely impossible; hence, where performance of the contract is merely more difficult than anticipated, or where the contract can be performed only at a time somewhat later than that specified for performance, the court will not refuse to make an enforcement order.[106]

474. In accordance with the traditional rule of equity, even where performance of the contract is possible, the court will not make an order for enforcement if enforcement consists in compelling the doing or acceptance of personal work or a personal service. Section 3(2) of the Remedies Law draws no distinction in this context between employment contracts and those involving an independent contractor, or between the doing of personal work or service and the acceptance thereof.

475. The exception articulated in section 3(2) is, however, subject to the provisions of section 22(b) of the Remedies Law which provides: 'The provisions of this law shall apply where no law regulating labour relations or any other law contains special provisions for the matter in question'. The general tendency to restrict the application of the exception is, evidenced by the formulation of section 3(2) itself. First, only those works or services which are essentially personal in nature will fall within the ambit of the exception. Hence, on several occasions the Supreme Court has ruled that a contractor does not provide a personal service;[107] nor will a service be considered personal where its performance is transferable to another.[108] Likewise, only work which is connected to the qualities and abilities of the individual employee will be deemed personal for the purposes of the exception. Second, section 3(2) does not refer to a particular kind of contract, but rather to the content of the enforcement order ('doing or acceptance'). Hence, it appears that the section does not bar the making of a restraining order (itself a means of enforcement according to the statutory definition mentioned above) in connection with a personal contract. Third, even within the framework of personal work or service contracts, section 3(2) will not bar the enforcement of contractual obligations which are not connected to the doing or acceptance of personal work or service, such as the payment of wages or salaries.

---

106. In such circumstances, the court may exercise its authority under s. 4 of the Remedies Law, discussed below, and make a conditional order of enforcement.
107. *See, e.g., Ofek v. Turikan* (1978) 33(1) PD 93, 98.
108. *Satam v. Markowitz* (1988) 44(1) PD 757, 765.

476. Where the work is of a personal nature, section 3(2) prevented the court, even in the case of an unfair dismissal, from enforcing the continuance of an employment contract.[109] While such a dismissal constitutes a fundamental breach of the contract, the injured party was restricted to a monetary remedy or to a declaration concerning the unfairness of the dismissal. This ruling was criticized for many years and indeed, in a dramatic turning point, the National Labour Court determined there is no justification not to enforce a labour contract where a permanent working relation and direct contact do not exist between an employee and an employer.[110]

477. The use by the courts of the third exception listed in section 3(3), i.e., unreasonable supervision on behalf of a court or execution office, has often been the object of criticism. Hence, in at least one case, an Israeli court avoided the application of this exception in the context of construction contracts by appointing a receiver to complete the performance of a contract for the building of an apartment.[111] Indeed, dicta exists to the effect that courts should refrain from exaggerating the difficulties involved in the required supervision.[112] The relevant considerations for the application of this exception are primarily the complexity of the contract, the anticipated duration of performance and the degree of cooperation required.[113]

478. The broadest and most important of the four exceptions to the right of enforcement is that which permits the court to refuse to grant enforcement if in the circumstances of the case granting this remedy would be unjust. The purpose of this exception is not to substitute compensation for enforcement whenever the former would constitute a proper remedy. Furthermore, justice is not an absolute concept but rather a relative concept requiring the courts to focus on the relation of the parties *inter se*, and on the circumstances of the particular case, in an effort to balance between the competing interests of the contracting parties.

479. In construing the concept of justice in the context of section 3(4), special consideration will be given to two factors: first, section 3(4) constitutes an exception to the general enforcement rule; second, the party claiming that enforcement is unjust is the party in breach of the contract. Both factors support a narrow interpretation of the concept, and a restrained application of the exception. The party in breach will have to persuade the court that, in the circumstances of the case (which include the circumstances existing at the time the contract was made, as well as subsequent circumstances), the injustice caused to him by enforcement will outweigh the injustice caused to the injured party, should he be forced to settle for compensation. In determining this issue, the courts will take into account, *inter alia*, the

109. However, where a collective agreement exists, imposing restrictions on dismissals, s. 3(2) will not prevent the enforcement of the agreement by means of a class action brought by the workers' association which is a party to the agreement: *Tzori v. Labour Court* (1974) PD 28(1) 372, 387.
110. *Mifalei Tachanot Ltd. v. Yaniv* (1996) 33 PDA 289.
111. *Unison v. Deutsch* (1976) 30(2) PD 398, 405.
112. *See, e.g., Tzdaka v. HaCohen* (1983) 37(4) PD 313, 321.
113. *Satam v. Markowitz* (*supra* note 109) 766.

conduct and interests of the parties, and the foreseeable consequences to each of them of enforcement and of non-enforcement.

IV. Conditions of Enforcement

480. Section 4 of the Remedies Law provides as follows:

> The court may make enforcement of the contract conditional upon fulfilment of the obligations of the injured party or upon assurance of their fulfilment or upon other conditions necessarily resulting from the contract in the circumstances of the case.

481. Section 4 does not constitute an additional exception to the right of enforcement, but instead empowers the court to issue a conditional enforcement order. Hence, in effect, the section supports the remedy of enforcement and the performance of contractual obligations.

482. In addition to conditions relating to the fulfilment of the injured party's obligations, or to an assurance of such fulfilment, the court may make enforcement of the contract dependent on other conditions 'necessarily resulting from the contract in the circumstances of the case'. This latter category has been construed as including only conditions having a close and material link to the contract and the breach thereof[114] – a limitation which is consistent both with the primacy accorded to the enforcement of the contract, and with the tendency to avoid excessive judicial intervention in contractual relations.

483. As a result of section 24 of the Remedies Law, which establishes the independence from English Law,[115] the cy-prés doctrine no longer forms part of Israeli law doctrine. According to this doctrine, in cases where exact enforcement is impossible, an injured party is entitled to the closest possible substitute to that which was promised him in the contract. However, the spirit and logic of this doctrine is consistent with the principle of good faith. Therefore, in circumstances in which the cy-prés doctrine would have applied, the principle of good faith will support issuing an enforcement order which corresponds to that which would have been made under the doctrine. Such an order will be made pursuant to section 4, which empowers the court to make an enforcement order 'conditional ... upon ... conditions necessarily resulting from the contract in the circumstances of the case'.

---

114. *Vinkler v. Safir Sodri* (1981) 36(2) PD 365, 375.
115. Section 24 of the Remedies Law provides: 'In matters dealt with by this law, article 46 of the Palestine Order in Council, 1922–1947, shall not apply.' Article 46 required Israeli courts to fill *lacunae* in Israeli law by reference to English law. Article 46 has now, in any case, been repealed by the Foundations of Law, 1980, s. 1 of which provides: 'Where the court, faced with a legal question requiring decision, finds no answer to it in statute law or case law or by analogy, it shall decide it in the light of the principles of freedom, justice, equity and peace of Israel's heritage.'

484. The authority granted to the court in section 4 of the Remedies Law, has been applied to enforce a contract on condition of revaluation of the sums owed by the injured party to the party in breach.[116] This approach allows the court to take into account the drop in the real value of the contract price, and to enforce the contract without thereby causing unjust harm to the party in breach. The rate of revaluation will be determined in accordance with the facts of each case, including the conduct of the parties following the making of the contact. However, revaluation will ordinarily fall short of full compensation for the drop in the real value of the contract price.

§5. Termination (Rescission)

I. Meaning of Rescission

485. The term 'rescission' is not defined in the Remedies Law. The term is not, however, to be understood as implying avoidance *ab initio*, as if the contract had never been made. Instead, rescission relieves both parties (i.e., the injured party as well as the party in breach) from performance of their respective future obligations under the contract; henceforth, each party is free to enter into new, alternative contracts.[117]

486. Although rescission severs the contractual link between the parties, the contract itself continues to play a role in the determination of the consequences of the breach, such as restitution and claims for compensation. Moreover, the contract may have included clauses regarding agreed compensation, arbitration or exemption from liability, which are not related to the active performance of the contract. In order to determine the validity and significance of such clauses it will be necessary to examine the validity and contents of the rescinded contract. Hence, rescission affects only the active, 'primary' obligations of the parties, and does so only as from the time of rescission.

II. Fundamental Breach

487. Section 6 of the Remedies Law provides as follows:[118]

> For the purpose of this article, 'fundamental breach' means a breach as to which it may be assumed that a reasonable person would not have entered into the contract had he foreseen the breach and its consequences, or a breach as to

116. The leading case is *Rabinai v. Mann Shaked* (1979) PD 33(2) 281.
117. Rescission in the event of a defect in consent or of a lack in substantive validity is discussed above at paras 250 et seq.
118. The term 'fundamental breach' in the present context is not to be confused with the English law doctrine of the same name governing the validity and scope of exemption clauses.

which it has been agreed in the contract that it shall be regarded as fundamental; a sweeping stipulation in a contract making breaches fundamental without differentiating between them is invalid unless it was reasonable at the time the contract was made.

488. Section 7(a) of the Remedies Law provides as follows:

> The injured party is entitled to rescind the contract if the breach thereof is fundamental.

489. By contrast, section 7(b) provides as follows:

> Where the breach of the contract is not fundamental, the injured party may rescind the contract if he has first given the person in breach an extension of time for performance and the contract has not been performed within a reasonable time after the giving of the extension.....

490. The crucial distinction between a breach which is fundamental and one which is not is as follows: while a fundamental breach entitles the injured party to rescind the contract immediately, the non-fundamental breach allows him to rescind only if the contract has not been performed within reasonable time after the extension has been given, subject to considerations of justice. Hence, where the breach is not fundamental, extension constitutes a prerequisite to the right to rescind.

491. In practice, however, an extension may and often will be given even in the case of a fundamental breach. In cases where the injured part is uncertain whether the breach is a fundamental one, granting an extension is recommended, as immediate rescission of the contract may result in the injured party himself breaching the contract. Furthermore, where in the case of a fundamental breach the injured party did not give notice of rescission within reasonable time after learning of the breach, as required by section 8 of the Remedies Law,[119] he may renew his right to rescind by first giving the party in breach an extension.[120]

492. The purpose of an extension is to grant the party in breach additional time to fulfil his contractual obligations and prevent rescission of the contract. While there are no formal, statutory requirements, concerning the manner in which an extension is to be given, notice of the extension must be clear and must reach the party in breach. What constitutes reasonable time for performance of the contract after extension has been given will depend on the circumstances of the case, and in particular on the kind of contract, the stipulations thereof, the time required for performance, and the financial-business background of the contract.

493. Section 6 distinguishes between two kinds of fundamental breach: an assumed fundamental breach and an agreed fundamental breach. The test applied

119. For further discussion, *see* paras 506–508.
120. *Margaliot v. Abarbanel* (1975) PD 29(2) 652, 657.

with respect to the first kind of fundamental breach is an objective one. It requires the court to examine both the breach and its consequences and to determine, in retrospect, whether or not a reasonable person – placed in the position of the injured party – who had foreseen the two at the time the contract was made, and nonetheless would have entered into the contract. Where the answer to this hypothetical question is negative, the breach is a fundamental one. However, the court will recognize a breach as fundamental only in extreme cases. The breach must have caused severe injury to the core of the contract, undermining its commercial basis, and depriving the injured party of the benefit he was supposed to have derived from the contract.

494. A fundamental breach will be assumed where no obligation of the contract has yet been performed by the party in breach, and this party has notified of his intention regarding the non-performance of his future contractual obligations. This will also be the case when a breach in relation to even one obligation will seriously affect the outcome of the injured party's expectations of the contract. Furthermore, it is possible that an accumulation of several breaches, none being fundamental on their own accord, will serve to undermine the confidence between the parties and thus be considered by the court as an assumed fundamental breach.

495. The consequences of the assumed fundamental breach referred to in section 6 include only the reasonable consequences of the breach and not the actual consequences.[121] Hence, in replying to the hypothetical question posed by the statutory definition, the court must confine itself to those consequences which were reasonably foreseeable at the time the contract was made, in view of the data available and known then.

496. The question whether delayed payment constitutes an assumed fundamental breach received conflicting answers in case law.[122] In resolving this issue objectively, the court will consider the duration of the delay in question, the relation between the amount not paid on time and the rest of the payments due under the contract as well as the conduct of the parties.

497. The second kind of fundamental breach described in section 6, an agreed fundamental breach, is based on the principle of freedom of contract. The agreement of the parties to regard a certain breach as fundamental is not subject to any test of reasonableness.

498. However, referring to an agreed fundamental breach section 6 also provides as follows: 'a sweeping stipulation in a contract making breaches fundamental without differentiating between them is invalid unless it was reasonable at the time the contract was made'. The burden of proof lies on the injured party to establish that the stipulation was reasonable at the time the contract was made, in view of the circumstances prevailing at the time. The fact that a sweeping stipulation is

121. *Biton v. Peretz* (1976) 30(1) PD 367 and 30(3) PD 581.
122. *Ibid.*, 371 (per Bernson J.); *Hershko v. Vekter* (1977) 31(2) PD 85, 98 (per Bernson J. as well).

held invalid will not affect the validity of a separate stipulation in the contract independently defining a particular breach as fundamental. Furthermore, such invalidity will have no bearing on the question whether a breach is fundamental according to the objective test applied with respect of an assumed fundamental breach.

III. Justice Qualification

499. According to section 7(b) of the Remedies Law, where the breach of the contract is not fundamental the injured party will not have the right to rescind if, in the circumstances of the case, rescission of the contract is unjust. The burden of proof concerning this issue is on the party in breach. In addition, the continuation of section 7(b) provides that 'the plea that rescission of the contract in unjust shall not be heard unless the person in breach opposes the rescission within a reasonable time after notice of rescission is given'. The purpose of this last provision is to prevent prolonged uncertainty concerning the validity of the contract and the rights of the parties.

500. The justice qualification in section 7(b) is similar to the exception to the right of enforcement based on justice in section 3(4) of the Remedies Law.[123] As in the case of section 3(4), in applying the test of justice in the context of rescission, the court will consider all the relevant circumstances of the particular case, including the interests and conduct of both parties.

IV. Partial Rescission

501. Section 7(c) of the Remedies Law provides as follows:

> Where the contract is severable into parts and one of the parts has been broken in a manner giving cause for rescission of that part, the injured party is only entitled to rescind the part which has been broken; if the breach constitutes also a fundamental breach of the whole contract, the injured party is entitled to rescind the part which has been broken or the whole contract.

502. According to section 9(b) of the Remedies Law, 'Where part of a contract has been rescinded, the provisions of sub-section 9(a) (relating to restitution after rescission)[124] shall apply to what the parties have received under that part.'

503. The question of whether or not a contract is severable into parts will depend on the particular circumstances of the case, and especially on the contents and structure of the contract. Section 19 of the General Contracts Law, discussed above,[125] allows for partial rescission where there has been a defect in the formation of the

123. Discussed above at para. 479.
124. Discussed above at paras 264–267 and below at paras 516–520.
125. Discussed above at paras 251–254, 270.

contract and, like section 9(b), employs the concept of severability. In spite of the similarity between these two sections, in the instance of a partial breach that amounts to a fundamental breach, the fact whether the contract may be severable bears no relevance. The injured party will be entitled to rescind the entire contract if he chooses to do so.

V. The Right to Rescind and Rescission Procedure

504. The right to rescind the contract is an autonomous right which can be exercised independently by the injured party by merely giving notice to the party in breach. Hence, the right to rescind implies a power: the power to change, unilaterally, the relation of the parties *inter se*.

505. The independent exercise of the right to rescind is not only sufficient for rescission, but it is also necessary. Rescission will not apply automatically by virtue of a breach of the contract. As long as the injured party does not exercise his right of rescission, the contract remains valid and binding. Hence, the injured party is entitled either to rescind the contract or to insist on its performance. The right to rescind must however be exercised in customary manner and in good faith.[126]

506. Section 8 of the Remedies Law provides as follows:

> Rescission of the contract shall be by notice by the injured party, within a reasonable time after he learnt of the breach, to the person in breach; however, in the case referred to in section 7(b) and in every other case in which the injured party has given an extension of time for performance of the contract, notice of rescission shall be given within a reasonable time after the extension of time has expired.

507. In order for notice of rescission to be valid, and to result in the rescission of the contract, the notice must conform to three requirements: form, contents and time.

508. While the Remedies Law itself stipulates no requirements of form, the notice must at least inform the person in breach of the rescission; mere knowledge of rescission gained by that person from some source other than the injured party, will not constitute valid notice. However, the notice need not be express. Conduct of the injured party from which an intention to rescind may be inferred, will constitute proper notice, provided such conduct is directed 'to the person in breach'.[127]

509. Section 21(a) of the Remedies Law provides as follows:

---

126. *Shalom v. Motta* (1982) 36(4) PD 793, 811.
127. *See, e.g., Kam v. Kam* (1984) 38(1) PD 767, 777.

> Notice under this law shall be given in the manner determined by the parties, and in the absence of such a determination, by registered post or in some other manner customary in the circumstances of the case.

510. It has been ruled that in certain cases the filing of a statement of claim will be deemed a 'customary manner' or notice.[128] However, this will not be the case where the contract itself establishes a special procedure for rescission.[129]

511. Section 21(b) of the Remedies Law provides as follows:

> An injured party who has given notice as provided in subsection (a) and who has reason to believe that the notice reached its destination in time may rely on it even if its arrival was delayed or it has not arrived at all.

512. With regard to the content of the notice of rescission it was held that the notice must clearly convey to the person in breach the injured party's intention to terminate their contractual relation.[130] However, conditional notice of rescission, giving the person in breach an opportunity to rectify the situation and including a warning that if he does not do so the contract will be rescinded, constitutes a proper notice of rescission.[131]

513. In the case of a fundamental breach (and assuming the injured party chooses not to give an extension), notice of rescission must be given within reasonable time after the injured party has learnt of the breach. Following the lapse of such time, the injured party will no longer be entitled to rescind, and the contract will remain valid. What constitutes reasonable time will be determined objectively in accordance with the special circumstances of each particular contract. Such circumstances will include the nature of the transaction, the substance of the contract, the periods indicated in the contract for the performance thereof and the conduct of the parties. Reasonable time will commence only after the injured party has actual knowledge of the breach. The source of such knowledge need not be the person in breach.

514. In the case of a breach which was not fundamental (or in the case of a fundamental breach where the injured party chooses to give an extension), reasonable time for notice will commence only after the required extension of time has expired. After the expiry of the extension, assuming the contract has not been performed, the injured party may rescind the contract. For this purpose, the injured party must give the person in breach a notice of rescission within reasonable time after the extension of time has expired.

---

128. *Car Hire Agencies v. Tarabloss* (1978) 33(1) PD 197, 202.
129. *Yosef v. Itzhaki* (1984) 38(3) PD 81, 83.
130. *Hechtmann v. Artzi* (1968) 22(2) PD 608, 612.
131. *Kadosh v. Amor* (1984) 38(2) PD 547, 556 (per Barak J.).

VI. Effect of Rescission

515. The rescission of a contract following a breach will affect the relation of the parties to the contract *inter se*, as well as the relation between such parties and third parties. With regard to third parties, the time of acquisition of a right by a third party is crucial: if such acquisition occurred prior to the breach, the third party has a strong and valid right to the asset. However, if the acquisition took place after the breach, the third party's right to the asset will prevail only if the third party acted in good faith and in the ordinary course of business.[132]

516. With regard to the relation of the contract parties *inter se*, section 9(a) of the Remedies Law provides as follows:

> Where the contract is rescinded, the person in breach shall restore to the injured party what he has received thereunder, or, if restitution is impossible or unreasonable or the injured party so chooses, shall pay him the value thereof; and the injured party shall restore to the person in breach what he has received under the contract, or, of restitution is impossible or unreasonable or the injured party so chooses, shall pay him the value thereof.

517. The obligation of restitution arises with and as a result of rescission. Once the injured party has rescinded he can choose between a claim for compensation or one for restitution, or even both, provided he does not receive a double remedy in respect of the same damage. However, while the purpose of compensation is to protect the expectation interest of the injured party, the purpose of restitution is to protect the restitution interest, and to prevent unjust enrichment.

518. The right to restitution, although established in the Remedies Law, does not emanate from the actual breach of the contract, but rather from its rescission. Moreover, in contrast to the other remedies that are only available to the injured party, restitution is obtainable by both parties.

519. Pursuant to section 9, each party must restore to the other 'what he has received' under the contract. Payment of the value that a party has received will be made only if restitution of the asset itself is impossible or unreasonable. In addition, the injured party has the option to choose payment of the value over actual restitution in respect of what he paid and what he received under the contract. Hence, in contrast to the arrangement of section 21 of the General Contracts Law, concerning rescission of a defective contract, the arrangement of section 9 is not symmetrical, but instead favours the injured party.

520. In times of inflation, unjust enrichment on the part of the party in breach will be prevented by requiring restitution of money paid under a contract to be made in accordance with the real, and not the nominal, value of the money. Hence, the

132. Compare para. 262 dealing with the effect of rescission on third parties in the event of a defect in consent or of a lack in substantive validity.

payment of linkage differentials will be required in such circumstances. Moreover, the Supreme Court has ruled that section 9 generally requires real restitution, including payment for the use of an asset or interest for the use of money.[133]

§6. Compensation (Damages)

I. Right to Compensation

521. The right to compensation derives from any breach of the contract. Where a contract has been breached compensation may be awarded in addition to the remedy of enforcement, or in addition to the remedy of rescission, or as a separate independent remedy. Compensation will be awarded in addition to enforcement where enforcement does not 'cure' the damage caused to the injured party, as, for example in the case of delayed payment. Compensation will be awarded in addition to rescission where rescission, together with restitution, does not cure the damage caused by the breach. Finally, compensation will be awarded as a separate remedy where the injured party either waives his right to the above other remedies, or is not entitled to them.

II. Aim of Compensation

522. The right to compensation, provided for in the Remedies Law, extends over two variants of losses caused to the injured party: expectation loss, caused to the positive interest and compensated by positive damages, and reliance loss, caused to the negative interest and compensated by negative damages. The main objective of compensation is to protect the expectation interest of the injured party by placing him in the position he would have been in, had the contract been performed and had the breach not occurred (*restitutio in intergrum*).[134] In contrast, reliance damages are granted in order to protect the reliance interest of the injured party. The objective of such damages is to place the injured party in the same position he occupied prior to the formation of the contract.[135]

523. The choice between the two variants of compensation lies with the injured party claiming for breach of the contract. However, the aim of compensation must be integrated with the basic presumption of the general remedies which are being claimed. Positive damages can only accompany the remedy of enforcement, while negative damages can only accompany the remedy of rescission. Independent compensation must be established on one basic presumption, be it positive or negative. The injured party can claim compensation as the only remedy in circumstances

133. *Amitey Malon Yerushalaim v. Taek* (1985) 40(3) PD 169, 211.
134. *Bank Igud v. Suraki* (1989) 42(4) PD 811; *United Mizrahi Bank Ltd. v. Lilof* (2001) 55(3) PD 200.
135. For further discussion regarding the protected interests, *see* the landmark article by Fuller & Perdue, *supra* note 48.

where he does not desire to rescind the contract but is not eligible for enforcement, or where he prefers monetary compensation.[136]

524. The aim of compensation, under Israeli law, is to compensate the injured party for damage caused to him, or for lost potential, and not to penalize the party in breach. Therefore, neither the Remedies Law nor case law makes any mention of punitive compensation – i.e., compensation which, due to the conduct of the party in breach, extends beyond that necessary to compensate the injured party for his loss and disheartened expectations, and aims at deterring similar conduct in the future. The accepted view is that compensation is to be awarded in strict accordance with the remoteness tests stipulated in the Remedies Law, and that Israeli courts have no authority to award either punitive or nominal damages.

III. Delimitation of Damage

525. In delimiting the damage, the court is concerned with determining the scope and extent of the damage for which the party in breach will be held liable. By contrast, in assessing the damage, such delimited damage will be converted into monetary figures in order to compensate the injured party.

526. Section 10 of the Remedies Law, which governs the delimitation of damage, provides as follows:

> The injured party is entitled to compensation for the damage caused to him by the breach and its consequences and which the person in breach foresaw or should have foreseen, at the time the contract was made, as a probable consequence of the breach.

527. This provision stipulates four cumulative conditions which must be met in order for the injured party to be entitled to the right to compensation due to breach of contract. First, damage caused by the breach. Second, causation between the damage and the breach. Third, foreseeability of the damage due to the breach. Fourth, the extent of the damage.

528. Section 10 lays down two delimitation tests: causation and foreseeability. The causation test restricts the application of the foreseeability test: In delimiting the damage, the court will first determine which damages were caused by the breach. Following the application of the causation test, the court will then determine, in relation to the damages caused by the breach, which damages were also foreseeable. Compensation will be awarded only in respect of such damages which pass both tests.

---

136. *Tzookim Hotel v. Natania's City Council* (1992) 46(4) PD 45, 74–78.

529. The existence of damage caused to the injured party is a prerequisite to an award of compensation. In the absence of damage, the existence of which must usually be established by the injured party,[137] no compensation will be awarded. Damages may include any harm to the person, personality or property of the injured party may be of pecuniary or non-pecuniary loss and be either direct or consequential.

530. After isolating the damage caused by the breach and its consequences, such damage will be subjected to the foreseeability test. The objective of this test is to allow the court to exercise its discretion in order to arrive at a result which is desirable in the circumstances of the case. Where the party in breach did not actually foresee the damage, it is for the court to determine what such party should have foreseen at the time the contract was made.

531. The following rules, established in the provisions of section 10, assist in the application of the foreseeability test:

(1) In contrast to the rule laid down in *Hadley v. Baxendale*,[138] the court is concerned only with what was foreseen or foreseeable by the party in breach, and not by the injured party.[139]
(2) Foreseeability is subject to an objective test – damage which a reasonable person is expected to have foreseen and expect, and will be assessed by court. Where the damage should have been foreseen it matters not whether it was in fact foreseen. Conversely, where the damage was in fact subjectively foreseen, it matters not whether it should have been foreseen.
(3) Foreseeability, both actual and potential, is determined in relation to the time the contract was made, and in accordance with the factual data known at the time, or which should have been known, to the party in breach. Hence, subsequent events will not be taken into account in applying the foreseeability test.
(4) Foreseeability relates to the damage caused by the breach, and not to the breach itself or to the manner in which the breach occurred. Therefore, compensation may, for example, be awarded for damages caused by unforeseen delays.
(5) Actual foresight has an objective aspect: compensation will be awarded against the party in breach in relation to damage foreseen as a probable, and not only as a certain, consequence of the breach. The objective determination of the probability of the damage resulting from the breach applies to both actual and potential foreseeability.

137. For two exceptions to this rule, *see* discussion concerning ss 11 and 15 of the Remedies Law at paras 545–561.
138. *Hadley v. Baxendale* (1854) 156 ER 145.
139. *Lubianiker v. Ministry of Finance* (1998) 56(5) PD 289, 298.

532. In a decision of the Supreme Court, the principle of foreseeability was employed so as to achieve revaluation of the compensation.[140] It was held that damage caused by a drop in the value of money was foreseeable and thus subject to compensation pursuant to section 10. This decision achieved harmony between the three contractual remedies: revaluation as against enforcement,[141] 'real' restitution in the case of rescission,[142] and revaluation of compensation.

533. Section 14(a) of the Remedies Law provides as follows:

> The party in breach shall not be liable to pay compensation under sections 10, 12, and 13 for damage which the injured party could have prevented or mitigated by reasonable measures.

534. The mere ability of the injured party to have prevented or reduced the damage, and not actual prevention or reduction, is sufficient to bar a claim for compensation in respect of the damage which could have been prevented or reduced. The principle of mitigation is based on both moral and economic considerations. The burden of proof concerning mitigation is on the party in breach.[143]

535. If follows from the formulation of section 14(a) that where the claim for compensation is not based on sections 10, 12 or 13 – but rather on section 11 (compensation without proof of damage) or 15 (agreed compensation) – it cannot be countered by the claim of mitigation. Since compensation under sections 11 and 15 is not based on damage actually caused, such compensation is not subject to the principle of mitigation.

536. 'Reasonable measures' in the context of section 14(a) will be determined in accordance with the facts of each particular case. Moreover, in determining this issue, the court will consider which measures were reasonable at the time of the breach, and not which measures it would have been reasonable to take in retrospect.

537. Section 14(b) of the Remedies Law provides as follows:

> Where the injured party has incurred reasonable expenses or undertook reasonable liabilities in order to prevent or mitigate damage, the party in breach shall indemnify him therefor, whether or not the damage was in fact prevented or mitigated; if the expenses or liabilities were unreasonable, the party in breach shall indemnify the injured party to the extent reasonable under the circumstances of the case.

538. As previously mentioned, the party in breach is exempt from compensation in respect of damage which could have been reasonably prevented or reduced,

140. *Berman v. Yair* (1981) 35(2) PD 701.
141. *See* para. 484.
142. *See* para. 520.
143. *Simhon v. Bechar* (1985) 39(1) PD 701, 708.

whether or not in fact prevented or reduced. Similarly, the party in breach is liable to indemnify the injured party in respect of reasonable expenses or liabilities incurred or contracted for the prevention or reduction of damage, whether or not the damage was in fact prevented or reduced. The burden of proof in the context of section 14(b) is on the injured party.

539. Section 14(b) further provides that indemnification for expenses incurred to mitigate the damage shall not exceed the amount considered as reasonable under the circumstances of the case. Therefore, the injured party will be indemnified only for the considered reasonable amount spent and not the surplus.

540. A second claim which serves to protect the party in breach is the defence of contributory negligence. Under the tort law doctrine of contributory negligence, a plaintiff's damages may be reduced on the grounds of his contributory negligence. This doctrine was adopted in Israeli contract law. The Supreme Court determined that the court is empowered to divide the liability between contracting parties when the good faith obligation has been breached.[144]

IV. Assessment of Damage

541. Following the delimitation of the damage for which the party in breach is liable, the next stage involves assessment of the damage in order to determine the measure of compensation to which the injured party is entitled in respect of the damage caused to him. At this stage, the damage caused to the injured party is translated into monetary figures. While the Remedies Law itself contains no test for determining the assessment of damage, the accepted rule is that damages are assessed by determining the sum of money which will place the injured party in the position he would have been in, had the contract been performed and the breach not occurred.[145]

542. The injured party claiming compensation within the framework of section 10 is entitled to full compensation for the damage caused to him. In addition to being required to prove the existence of damage, the injured party must also prove the measure of compensation.[146] However, in cases where precise proof of the appropriate measure of compensation is difficult, it will be sufficient for the injured party to supply general data proving the extent of the damage within reasonable degree of certainty.[147] The court, in the exercise of its discretion, will complete the assessment. In assessing the damage, the court is not restricted to the date of the breach, the date of rescission, or any other date.[148] The damage assessed by the court will also include loss of profits.

144. *Eximin v. Textile and Footwear* (n 113).
145. *Yetzirot Bernea v. Dania Chevrah LePituach* (1988) 42(2) PD 793, 798.
146. *Anisimov v. Malon Tirat Bat-Sheva* (1981) 35(2) PD 800, 806.
147. *Ibid.*, 809.
148. *Ibid.*, 800.

543. Section 13 of the Remedies Law provides as follows:

Where the breach of contract has caused other than pecuniary damage, the court may award compensation for that damage at the rate it deems appropriate in the circumstances of the case.

544. In contrast to cases involving pecuniary damage, the injured party does not have a vested right to compensation for non-pecuniary damage; rather, such compensation is awarded, if at all, at the court's discretion. The reason for this distinction lies in the difficulty involved in quantifying non-pecuniary damage. Non-pecuniary damage will include pain and suffering, distress and possibly also loss of enjoyment. Within the context of non-pecuniary damage, the burden is on the injured party to prove the existence of the damage, as well as the causal nexus between the damage and the breach. Thereafter, his claim will be subject to the court's discretion. Although section 13 does not explicitly demand foreseeability of damage, the Supreme Court has unequivocally determined that the requirement applies to non-pecuniary damages as well.[149] However, non-pecuniary damages are rarely ruled and if they are, very modest compensation is awarded.

545. Section 11 of the Remedies Law provides as follows:

> (a) Where an obligation to supply or receive any property or service has been breached and the contract is rescinded by reason of the breach, the injured party shall, without proof of damage, be entitled to compensation in the amount of the difference between the consideration for the property or service under the contract and its value on the date of rescission of the contract.
> (b) Where an obligation to pay a sum of money has been broken, the injured party shall, without proof of damage, be entitled to compensation in the amount of the interest on the sum in arrears from the date of the breach to the date of payment, at the full rate under the Adjudication of Interest Law, 1961, unless the Court has prescribed a different rate.

546. Section 11 mentions two classes of cases in which the injured party may receive compensation without proof of damage: breach of an obligation to supply or receive any property or service and breach of an obligation to pay a sum of money.

547. Both subsections of section 11 determine a standard rate of compensation characteristic of the obligation in question. In both cases the damage is apparent from the breach itself and thus requires no proof. Moreover, the injured party basing his claim within the framework of section 11 is exempt from proving causation of the damage and foreseeability, nor is he under an obligation to mitigate the damage.

548. According to section 12 of the Remedies Law 'The provisions of section 11 shall not derogate from the right of the injured party to compensation proved

149. *Goldman v. Michaeli* (1981) 35(4) PD 31, 41.

under section 10; … '. Hence, the injured party may choose to base his claim within the framework of section 10, or even within the framework of both sub-sections of section 11, alternatively or jointly.

549. The assumption underlying the compensation rule in section 11(a) is that the injured party – following rescission of the contract – will arrange for an alternative transaction in accordance with the value of the property or service. Hence, the section makes provision for a simple arithmetical calculation based on the difference between the contractual consideration and the value of the property or service on the date of rescission. This value will usually be determined according to the market value of the product or service. However, where no such market is available, alternative yardsticks must be adopted as, for example, production costs in the case of the breach of a contract of sale by the purchaser. A claim for compensation pursuant to section 11(a) requires rescission of the contract.

550. The assumption underlying the compensation rule in section 11(b) is that interest represents the price for the use of money, while the period of arrears is the period during which the injured party was prevented from making such use. Where the interest which may be awarded under section 11(b) does not represent the actual loss sustained by the injured party as a result of the breach (e.g., the injured party was forced to borrow money at the market rate of interest), he may bring his claim under section 10 and prove his actual loss. A claim for compensation pursuant to section 11(b) does not require rescission of the contract and therefore may be claimed together with the claim of enforcement. Section 11(b) empowers the court to prescribe a rate of interest other than the full rate under the Adjudication of Interest Law, 1961, and in this way to ensure 'real' compensation.[150]

551. Section 15(a) of the Remedies Law, addresses the topic of agreed compensation and provides as follows:

> Where the parties have agreed in advance on the rate of compensation … compensation shall be as agreed, without proof of damage; however, the court may reduce the compensation if it finds that it was fixed without any reasonable relation to the damage which could be foreseen, at the time the contract was made, as a probable consequence of the breach.

552. The validity of a stipulation for agreed compensation derives from the principle of freedom of contract. The injured party relying on such a stipulation need not prove damage (*a fortiori*: he need not prove causation or foreseeability), nor is his claim subject to the obligation concerning mitigation of damages or contributory negligence.

553. Agreed compensation according to section 15(a) must be agreed upon prior to the breach of the contract, although it can be in a separate agreement. It may also be agreed in relation to a breach of a non-contractual obligation, such as a tortious

150. *Iryat Netanyah v. 'Sachaf'* (1986) 40(3) PD 235, 244.

action. Furthermore, agreed compensation need not be in monetary value, but may merely stipulate the method of calculation, e.g., a certain percentage of the contract value.

554. The application of section 15(a), and the validity of an agreed compensation stipulation, is dependent on the interpretation of both the contract containing the stipulation and the stipulation itself, in accordance with the ordinary rules of contractual interpretation based on the intention of the parties.

555. The power granted to the court to reduce the amount of compensation agreed upon constitutes an exception to the broad rule validating such stipulations, and for this reason will be exercised sparingly, i.e., only in exceptional circumstances where no reasonable relation exists between the agreed compensation and the foreseeable damage.[151] In determining whether to exercise its power to reduce agreed compensation, the court will compare such compensation with the damage which was foreseeable, at the time the contract was made, as a probable consequence of the actual breach in question. The court will assess whether, at the time the contract was made, the parties would have viewed the agreed compensation as reasonably reflecting the damage likely to be caused – i.e., not the damage in fact caused – by the actual breach.

556. The following rules concerning the application of the court's power to reduce agreed compensation may be derived from the relevant case law:

(1) The court is not empowered, in an appropriate case, to annul the agreed compensation stipulation, but only to reduce the agreed sum.
(2) The test the court must apply upon reducing agreed compensation is whether a reasonable person, placed in the shoes of the party to the contract, could have, at the time the compensation was agreed upon, considered the amount as befitting the damage rate due to be caused upon the breach of contract. A negative answer will empower the court to reduce the agreed compensation.
(3) Although section 15, in contrast to section 10, does not explicitly stipulate that foreseeability of damage be by the party in breach, it seems that foreseeability of damage in the context of section 15(a) must also be considered in regard to the party in breach.
(4) The reduction will reflect a reasonable relation between the compensation and the foreseeable damage. However, since the court will exercise its authority in this context sparingly, the actual compensation awarded will correspond to the upper limit of the sum reasonably reflecting the foreseeable damage.
(5) The court will focus on the actual breach, its circumstances and severity. The foreseeable damage rate – and thus the rate of agreed compensation – will be greater in the case of a fundamental breach than in the case of a less severe breach.
(6) The actual rate of reduction will depend on the circumstances of the case and the contract in question.

---

151. *Goldstein v. Gov Ari* (1984) 38(1) PD 309, 319.

(7) The test disregards the actual damage caused by the breach, but rather considers whether the agreed compensation determined is within reasonable relation to foreseeable damage caused by such a breach. An agreed compensation stipulation determining the same compensation in respect of any breach of the contract is, prima facie, unreasonable. A stipulation of this kind suggests that the parties did not actually consider the relation between the agreed compensation and the foreseeable damage. However, in contrast to a sweeping stipulation making breaches fundamental without differentiating between them (which is invalid, according to the second part of section 6 of the Law), a sweeping stipulation concerning agreed compensation will not be invalid, but only subject to the court's power of reduction.

(8) The burden of proof regarding an 'unreasonable relation' is on the party in breach, who must expressly raise and establish this claim.

557. Section 15(b) of the Remedies Law provides as follows:

> An agreement as to agreed compensation shall not by itself derogate from the right of the injured party to claim compensation under sections 10 to 14 in lieu thereof or from any other remedy for breach of contract.

558. The words 'by itself' in the above provision attest to the parties' right to restrict the application of sections 10–14, as well as the application of other contractual remedies. Where, however, such right has not been exercised the mere fact of agreed compensation will not have this effect. Section 15(b) enables the injured party to choose between agreed compensation or – in lieu thereof – a claim for compensation under sections 10–14. The advantage of a claim under section 10 as opposed to a claim for agreed compensation is that such a claim will not be confined to the agreed amount, nor will it be subject to the court's power to reduce agreed compensation. However, under section 10 the injured party will have to prove damage, causation and foreseeability, and to mitigate his damages. Unless otherwise agreed, the injured party will be entitled to agreed compensation together with any other remedy for breach of contract, i.e., he will not have to choose between either one of them.

559. Although the injured party, by virtue of section 15(b), is entitled to claim for agreed compensation together with other remedies, he will not be entitled to claim for duplication of remedies pertaining to the same damage.[152]

560. Section 15(c) of the Remedies Law provides as follows:

> (c) For the purposes of this article, sums which the party in breach paid to the injured party before the breach and which the parties agreed in advance should be forfeited to the injured party are deemed to be agreed compensation.

---

152. *Huri v. Israel Electricity Company Ltd.* (1991) 46(1) PD 115.

561. The effect of this provision is that contractual forfeiture arrangements will henceforth be treated by the court as agreed compensation, and will therefore be governed and restricted by the same rules applicable in the context of agreed compensation, including the court's power to reduce such compensation.

Part II. Specific Contracts

Chapter 1. Agency

§1. Introduction

562. The agency relationship in Israel is governed by the Agency Law, 1965. This law constitutes an original Israeli product, repealing English and Turkish laws that were in force prior to its enactment. The law contains several innovative arrangements, such as those pertaining to unauthorized agency and to undisclosed agency. The law applies continental models as well as Anglo-American common law. However, the language and terms of the law are derived primarily from Jewish law.

563. The Agency Law extends mainly to agency by will. Agency is a trilateral relationship. At its foundation is the relationship between a principal and an agent, alongside the relationship between the principal and third party on the one hand, and the relation between the agent and the third party on the other hand. The Agency Law adopts the common law model, according to which an agency comprises of a system of special rules and deals with the internal relationship between the principal and the agent, as well as the relationship between them and the third party. However, the relationship between the principal and the agent is only dealt with generally, on the assumption that the details of the relationship will be more specifically arranged in accordance with the particular context of the relationship, e.g., labour relations, contractor's relations, etc.

§2. Model Adopted

564. Whereas the continental system distinguishes between direct agency (where the third party is aware of the identity of the principal) and indirect agency (where the third party does not know who the principal is), and the English system draws no such distinction, Israeli law has adopted an intermediate approach. According to section 7 of the Agency Law, when the agent does not disclose the fact that he is acting as an agent, his act binds both himself and the principal, thus creating, as under common law principles, a direct relationship between the principal and a third party. However, while the act of the agent entitles the agent, it does not vest any right directly in the principal. Yet, the principal may adopt the rights vested in his agent as against the third party, subject to limitations deriving from the nature of the right, its conditions or the circumstances of the case. This approach resembles the approach of continental systems.

§3. Other Laws That Are Applicable

565. Although the Agency Law specifically governs the agency, other laws will also apply. When agency is created by a contract, the General Contracts Law will be applied. For example, when the principal notifies the agent of the cancellation of the agency, this will often be considered a breach of contract, and the agent will be entitled to sue for the remedies subject to the Remedies Law. However, according to section 14(a) of the Agency Law, the agency terminates upon cancellation by the principal, thus the injured agent will not be entitled to receive the remedy of enforcement.

§4. Theoretical Basis

566. The institute of agency is based on the principle according to which legal actions of the agent towards the third party establish a direct legal relationship between the principal and the third party.

567. The Agency Law does not adopt the 'identification theory', which creates a fictitious identity between the agent and principal. Nor does it adopt the 'contract theory', according to which the act of the agent binds and entitles the principal, since the expression of will of the principal towards his agent, or towards the third party, creates a contract between him and the third party. Former Chief Justice Prof. A. Barak, in his leading commentary on the Agency Law, maintains that the theory upon which the Israeli law rests is the 'theory of power'. According to this theory, authorization is defined as the conferral of power to the agent, allowing him to perform a legal action on behalf of the principal. Section 1 of the Agency Law establishes the principle that the agent has the power to change the legal rights and obligations of the principal towards a third party by virtue of his actions. The agent's power derives from the principal, by the expression of the principal's will towards the agent or the third party. This theory explains why the agent must have legal capacity, namely because he is conferred with power that enables him to bind and entitle the principal. The theory of power also explains the ability of the principal to ratify an act 'ex post facto', as well as the binding of the principal by an undisclosed agency. The principal empowers his agent so that if the third party does not know of the agency or of the identity of the principal, the principal becomes obligated towards the third party.

§5. Basic Rules

568. The Agency Law establishes specific rules for agency, yet it does not deal with the rights and obligations vested in the parties pursuant to the contract between them, which is subject to the General Contracts Law. Furthermore, the law includes no provisions concerning the relationship between the agent, operating within his scope of authorization, and the third party. It is thus possible that a contract will be created between the agent and the third party, in which the former will be liable towards the latter.

569. The Agency Law establishes an obligation of trust that binds the agent towards the principal, entitling the latter, upon its infringement, to the remedies pursuant to a breach of contract.

570. Some basic rules of agency provided for in the Agency Law may be summarized as follows:

(1) Agency generally – and not merely 'agency by estoppel' – is created by the expression of the principal's will.
(2) The third party may refuse to recognize the agency as long as a written authorization has not been produced.
(3) When the agent acts beyond the scope of his authorization, the third party may regard him as a party to the act, or withdraw from the act and claim damages from the agent.
(4) A corporate body may ratify an act performed on its behalf prior to its establishment.
(5) In an undisclosed agency, the act of the agent binds the agent and principal jointly and severally, but entitles the agent only. The principal may assume the agent's right.
(6) The infringement of the trust obligation between agent and principal entitles the injured principal to remedies for breach of contract (section 9). If the third party is privy to the infringement, the principal has the right to repudiate the agent's act, and claim compensation from the third party.
(7) The agent holds any property that comes into his possession in consequence of the agency as a trustee of the principal.

§6. Basic Principles

571. The Agency Law is based on the following basic principles:

(1) The fulfilment of the reasonable expectations of the parties:
The rule by which the act of the agent binds and entitles the principal serves to fulfil the parties' reasonable expectations. When the third party has no knowledge of the agency, his expectation is that the agent he is communicating with will be the party to whom he is legally bound. The law acknowledges this expectation, and hence, when the right administered by the third party to the agent is non-transferable, it remains with the agent, and the principal may not claim it himself. When the agent acts beyond the scope of his authorization the law entitles the third party to compensation from the agent. In addition, the law

provides that if the agency is terminated without the knowledge of the agent, or the third party, they may both consider it as still effective.

(2) The agent carries the risk of an unauthorized action:

In the relationship between the principal and the third party the risks of an unauthorized act are borne by the third party and if the agent acts beyond the scope of his authorization, his act does not bind or entitle the principal. However, the third party may transfer the risk on to the agent, pursuant to section 6(b) which entitles him to view the agent as his party to the act, or to claim damages from him. If the agency is terminated without the knowledge of the third party, he may regard it as valid so that even if the agent acts without authorization his action will bind and entitle the principal. However, the principal may pass the risk on to the agent, since an unauthorized act by the agent may be considered an infringement of the agent's obligation of trust. In this case the principal will be entitled to remedies from the agent. The only case in which the agent will not bear the risk is when he is not aware of the termination of the agency. In this case the agency may be regarded as valid and the principal will, therefore, bear the risk.

(3) The protection of those who act in good faith:

A party who acts in good faith, and is unaware of the lack of authorization, is not deprived of his rights. In addition, the law establishes that a ratification 'ex post facto' shall not impair any right acquired by another person in good faith and for consideration.

Chapter 2. Bailment

§1. Introduction

572. The Bailees Law, 1967, applies to contract, tort and property law. The law is an independent Israeli creation, based on both Jewish law and provisions characteristic of continental legal systems.

573. In fact, the law deals with various types of arrangements, including those based on commercial relationships, as well as those based on friendly and informal ones. The law applies to bailment created by agreement in addition to those created by law. The creation of other legal relations may lead to the creation of a bailment e.g., the creation of a pledge will give rise to a bailment upon the deposition of the pledged property. In short, the institution of bailment applies in the context of various sets of legal relationships and obligations. Accordingly, the provisions of the Bailees Law shall apply to the bailment of property where no special provisions applicable to the matter exist in any other law and no contrary intention appears from the agreement between the parties.

§2. The Nature of Bailment

574. The Bailees Law governs the relationships between the bailee and the owner of the bailed property. It defines the duties and rights of both parties, imposes certain rules of conduct on the bailee and most importantly, determines the nature and scope of the bailee's liability for the loss or damage to the bailed property. The main provisions of the law deal with the distribution of rights to the bailed property as between the owner and the bailee, the distribution of responsibility for the safekeeping of the bailed property and the allocation of risk for loss or damage caused to the property. The law may therefore be classified as constituting part of the law of property.

575. The Bailees Law does not deal with the contractual relationship which may exist between the parties and which will therefore be governed by the provisions of the General Contracts Law and Remedies Law, as in the case of any other agreement. The parties to a bailment agreement may choose to contract out of the provisions of the law. However, a bailment may be created without the need for an agreement between the bailee and the bailor, e.g., where a person becomes a bailee by virtue of having found lost property. A bailment may also follow upon the creation of certain property rights, such as those by a lease or a pledge.

576. Section 1(a) of the Bailees Law defines the Israeli institution of bailment system as follows, 'holding property by way of bailment is the lawful possession thereof, otherwise than by virtue of ownership'. Three elements may be discerned in this definition: the possession of property, the lawful nature of that possession and the exclusion of possession by virtue of ownership.

577. With respect to the first element of the definition of a bailment, the possession of property, the term 'possession', is usually interpreted as implying the existence of control over the property in question, combined with the intention of having such control. These two elements, control and the relevant intention, justify the bailee's duty to safekeep the bailed property, as well as the imposition of liability on the bailee if he or she fails to do so. However, not every set of circumstances in which a person obtains, by way of agreement, possession of property belonging to another will necessarily give rise to a bailment. The agreement between the parties must be intended to create a bailment by virtue of which the party in possession will be responsible for the safekeeping of the property. The creation of such an arrangement must be one of the primary goals of the agreement.

578. The bailee must have lawful possession of the property. The law defines the owner of the bailed property as any person for whom the bailee holds the property. Hence, if the bailee has received possession of the property pursuant to an agreement and not by a wrongful act, his possession will be regarded as lawful even if the consent of the person in whom ownership is actually vested has not been obtained. Unlawful possession by the 'owner' – as defined in the law – will not undermine the lawful nature of the bailee's possession where he has received such possession by virtue of the 'owner's' will. Only if the bailee has received possession from the owner by means of a wrongful act will such possession be considered unlawful.

579. The third element in the definition of bailment is that possession be otherwise than by virtue of ownership. The possession of property as an owner thereof will not be considered a bailment, but rather a natural consequence of ownership. Hence, the bailee may never be the owner of the bailed property, although he may have certain property rights therein, such as in the case of a hire or pledge.

§3. Different Types of Bailees

580. The law recognizes four types of bailees: gratuitous bailee, bailee for reward, bailee for reward when the purpose of safekeeping is subordinate to the principal purpose of the possession and borrower. All bailees will be classified into one of these four types.

581. The liability of the bailee for loss or damage to the property shall vary in accordance with the classification of the bailee. With regard to liability, the pivotal concept in all four classifications is that of benefit: the benefit received by the bailee by virtue of the bailment, in addition to benefit thus received by the owner. In this regard, the liability of a gratuitous bailee is less severe than that of the bailee for reward since the latter will have received consideration for the bailment, a factor justifying a rise in the level of his liability.

582. The benefit received by the bailee for the bailment does not need to be financial. Such benefit may also include any non-material benefit awarded on account of the bailment. The concern pertaining to whether or not a benefit was received by the bailee will be determined in accordance with the intention of the parties and the general circumstances of the bailment. The parties must intend that some benefit be received by the bailee in consequence of the bailment. Usually when the relationship between the parties is a commercial one, this will indicate that the bailee is a bailee for reward. However, in the case of a friendly relationship the natural assumption will be that the bailee is a gratuitous bailee or borrower, according to the circumstances.

583. A gratuitous bailee is one who derives no benefit from the bailment. In such case, the owner alone derives benefit from the bailment without rewarding the bailee; hence, the liability of the gratuitous bailee for loss or damage to the property is the least severe: the gratuitous bailee will be liable only if the loss or damage is caused through his negligence.

584. A bailee for reward is a bailee who receives consideration or derives some other benefit from the bailment, and who is not a borrower. In this instance, the benefit from the bailment is mutual to both the bailee and the owner. The owner's property is bailed, and the bailee receives some benefit as a result. The benefit received by the bailee justifies the imposition of a stricter level of liability than that imposed on the gratuitous bailee. Accordingly, a bailee for reward is liable for loss or damage to the property unless it has been caused by circumstances which he need not have foreseen and the consequences of which he could not have averted.

585. A special type of bailee for reward is established when the purpose of the safekeeping is subordinate to the principle purpose of the possession, as for example, in the case of a pledge or hire. The position adopted by law is that in such circumstances the liability of the bailee should be of a lesser degree than when the safekeeping is the primary goal of the possession by the bailee. Accordingly, in such circumstances the bailee will be exempt from liability if the loss or damage is caused otherwise than through his negligence. While the liability imposed on this kind of bailee for reward will therefore be similar to the level of liability imposed on the gratuitous bailee, a difference exists concerning the burden of proof. In the former case, in contrary to the latter, the burden of proof will be on the bailee to establish the absence of negligence on his part.

586. The fourth type of bailee is the borrower, who is given the right to use or enjoy the property without giving consideration. Accordingly, his liability is the strictest among the various types of bailees – a borrower is liable for any loss or damage whatever its cause, provided that his liability shall not be more stringent than that of unlawful possessor. For example, the borrower would not be responsible for loss or damage resulting from force majeure.

587. The law establishes certain exceptions to the different types and degrees of liability. First, if a bailee is aware of damage for which he is not usually liable, which is likely to be caused to the property, and does not notify the owner of this fact within reasonable time or does not take reasonable measures to notify the owner, he shall be liable for the damage caused, which his notification would have prevented.

588. A further case of a more stringent liability created by law is where a gratuitous bailee, or bailee for reward, having received any property for his or her personal safekeeping, delivers it to another person without being explicitly or implicitly authorized to do so. In such a case, the degree of liability for any loss or damage to the property shall be that of a borrower.

589. The bailee will be exempt from liability for the loss or damage to the property caused by ordinary use thereof in accordance with the conditions of the bailment, by natural deterioration, or by defect existing therein at the commencement of the bailment.

§4. Remedies in the Bailees Law

590. Where the bailee is liable for the loss or damage to the property, the owner of the property shall be entitled to compensation for breach of contract. In circumstances where the bailee is not liable but has a right to compensation or indemnification for such loss or damage against a third party, the owner of the property may claim his damage from the bailee in respect of the compensation or indemnification due to the bailee. The purpose of this latter provision is to prevent unjust enrichment. The compensation due to the bailee is awarded in consequence of his duties as a bailee. However, he is exempt from liability for the loss or damage to the property, such loss or damage being borne by the owner of the property. Therefore, in order to prevent the unjust enrichment of the bailee, he is under an obligation to share the received compensation with the owner.

591. The owner of the property is under an obligation to indemnify a gratuitous bailee, as well as the holder of a pledge or other security, for reasonable expenses incurred and liabilities reasonably contracted in consequence of the bailment. Moreover, the law entitles the bailee to perform any urgent and unforeseen act reasonably required in order to prevent damage likely to be caused to the property, as though the owner of the property had authorized him to do so. The bailee will also be entitled to indemnification for the expenses incurred in consequence of any such act performed by him.

Chapter 3. Gaming and Wagering

§1. Introduction

592. Section 32(a) of the General Contracts Law states that gambling, lottery or betting contracts are unenforceable, both directly (by way of enforcement) and indirectly (by way of compensation). An examination of this section, in light of policy considerations, reveals the reason for its operative provision. The legal system's attitude to gambling, lottery or betting contracts ranges from lack of sympathy to condemnation and hostility.

593. This attitude results from a range of psychological, sociological and economic factors. Betting has always been – and still is – considered a private and social plague. It results in a loss of time, wasted money and sometimes even poverty. It creates anti-social attitudes and unethical values among the participants. The acquisition of money as a result of pure luck and not as a result of personal labour or effort, may lead to demoralization and idleness.[153] Betting in particular, but also lotteries and gambling, encourage unsocial desires for quick and easy enrichment and cause waste and squandering. In economic terms, gambling, lottery or betting contracts create new risks which arise from contracts.

594. These factors are the source of the hostility towards gambling inherent in section 32 and in certain provisions of criminal law which prohibit gambling, lotteries or betting.[154] The approach of section 32 is a paternalistic one, intended to protect members of the public from themselves and from their deficiencies and to protect the entire public from betting and lotteries by restricting the freedom of contract.

§2. The Provisions of Section 32(a)

595. Section 32(a) of the General Contracts Law provides as follows:

> A gambling, lottery or betting contract under which a party may win some benefit, the winning being depending on fate, guesswork of a chance occurrence more than on understanding or ability, is not actionable and does not give rise to compensation.

596. This provision is divided into three distinct elements:

(1) The type of contract in question – a 'gambling, lottery or betting contract under which a party may win some benefit'.

---

153. *See* the sharp and hostile depiction of the 'plague' of lotteries and betting in *Savitsky v. Minister of Finance*, (1965) 19(2) PD 369, 376–377.
154. *See* ss 224–235 of the Penal Law, 1977 (LSI Special Volume).

(2) Its criterion – 'the winning being dependent on fate, guesswork or a chance occurrence rather than on understanding or ability'.
(3) Its consequences – 'is not actionable and does not give rise to compensation'.

597. Following this threefold division, the three following elements are to be considered:

(1) The definition of a gambling lottery or betting contract.
(2) The criterion for definition – namely, the relatively test.
(3) The consequences of a gambling, lottery or betting contract.

§3. The Definition of a Gambling, Lottery or Betting Contract

598. A gambling contract is a contract under which a party stands to gain some benefit subject to the outcome of a game, when such a result depends more on chance than on the understanding or skills of the party. A lottery contract is a contract under which a party may gain benefit contingent on fate or otherwise. A betting contract is a contract under which a party's win is dependent on the prediction or guesswork of the result of a specific act or the occurrence of a certain event.[155]

§4. The Relativity Test

599. The relativity test, embodied in the words 'rather than', restricts the definition of the contract predicated in section 32(a). In order for a contract to be unenforceable it is not sufficient for it to be merely a gambling, lottery or betting contract – a further condition is that the win be dependent on fate, guesswork or a chance occurrence more than on understanding or ability. This test is not simple to implement. Its criterion is objective and general, requiring the individual examination of each form of gambling, lottery or betting in accordance with its particular rules and circumstances.

600. The relativity test in section 32 assumes that gambling, lotteries and betting lie between two extremes. At one extreme are those forms of gambling, lotteries and betting in which success depends on understanding or ability. Chess tournaments, football matches, sporting meets and quizzes of knowledge fall within this category and are certainly beyond the scope of section 32. At the other extreme are those forms of gambling, lotteries and betting, such as roulette and bingo, in which success depends entirely on luck and are obviously within the scope section 32. Within this range are games in which there is a clear element of luck, although understanding or skill is also required – for example, certain card games which start with an arbitrary dealing of the cards but afterwards necessitate some degree of

155. Cf. the definitions in s. 224 of the Penal Law, 1977. However, these definitions do not include the term 'contract'.

knowledge or understanding. In accordance to the test of relativity, it will be necessary to discern the dominant factor in relation to such games – chance or skill. The answer will differ from one case to the next, since each gambling, lottery or betting contract will be considered under its particular circumstances.

§5. The Consequences of Gambling, Lottery or Betting Contracts

I. General

601. The suffix of section 32(a) prescribes the effect of a gambling, lottery or betting contract. Such a contract 'is not actionable and does not give rise to compensation'.

602. The penal regulation of forbidden games, lotteries and betting is provided in sections 224–235 of the Penal Law 1977. This regulation requires that a distinction be made between gambling, lottery or betting contracts prohibited by criminal law and those that do not fall within the scope of the aforementioned penal provisions. A gambling, lottery or betting contract as provided by the Penal Law is an illegal contract as defined by section 30 of the General Contracts Law and is therefore void and subject to section 31 of the law. It may, therefore, be concluded that both subsections of section 32 concern gambling, lottery and betting contracts which for various reasons do not fall within the ambit of sections 30 and 31 of the General Contracts Law, which deal with illegal contracts.

603. Hence, the proposed distinction between three categories of gambling, lottery and betting contracts is as follows:

(1) Illegal gambling, lottery and betting contracts which are subject to sections 30 and 31 of the General Contracts Law.
(2) Unenforceable gambling, lottery and betting contracts which are subject to and regulated by section 32(a) of the General Contracts Law.
(3) Contracts concerning gambling, lotteries and betting regulated by law or for the conduct of which a permit has been issued under any law; such contracts are permitted and, in according to section 32(b), they are subject to the General Contracts Law.

II. Illegal Gambling, Lottery or Betting Contracts

604. The first category of illegal contracts, namely gambling, lottery or betting contracts, should be addressed within the framework of sections 30–31 of the General Contracts Law, which deal with illegal contracts. A gambling, lottery or betting contract prohibited by criminal law is void according to section 30. However, section 31 applies the rules of restitution to such a void contract, and further provides that a party to an illegal contract may be required to fulfil its (ostensibly void) contractual obligations.

605. It appears that in light of section 32, which denies the remedies of enforcement and damages in the case of gambling, lottery or betting contracts, the court will not be inclined to require a party to an illegal gambling, lottery or betting contract to fulfil its obligation even if the other party has fulfilled his corresponding commitment. In other words, the provision of section 32, which concerns gambling, lottery or betting contracts which are not illegal, restricts the discretion of the court when it considers gambling.

606. However, section 32 does not deny the remedy of restitution from a party to a gambling, lottery or betting contract and also applies to such contracts that fall within the scope of section 30.

III. Unenforceable Gambling, Lottery or Betting Contracts

A. The Rule

607. The second category is that of gambling, lottery or betting contracts, which are not illegal but are subject to section 32(a) which determines their unenforceability. Amongst these are gambling, lottery or betting contracts which, in accordance with section 230 of the Penal Law, do not contain a criminal element provided the following three conditions are met:

(1) Their conduct is intended for a particular circle of persons.
(2) They do not exceed the scope of amusement or entertainment.
(3) They are not conducted at a venue for prohibited games or for the conduct of lotteries or betting.

B. Enforcement and Damages

608. The main objective of section 32(a) is the denial of the remedies of enforcement and damages from a party to a gambling, lottery or betting contract. Consequently, it is not possible to claim enforcement for the performance of a gambling game for which the organizer undertook to conduct. Similarly, it is not possible to enforce the conduct of a lottery, just as the results of a bet cannot be enforced. These contracts are unenforceable both directly and indirectly by means of compensation.

609. The *ratio legis* of section 32(a) is clear. Since the legislator's attitude pertaining to the contracts in question is unsympathetic, the judicial system will not facilitate their existence, by providing to the injured party the usual remedies upon breach.

C. Rescission and Restitution

610. Section 32(a) denies the remedies of enforcement and damages to a party to a gambling, lottery or betting contract. However, a party to such a contract is still entitled to rescission. Rescission differs from enforcement and damages in that it can usually be effectuated by self-help. The remedy of rescission arises in the case of defects in the formation of the contract, in accordance with Chapter 2 of the General Contracts Law, and in the case of breach, in accordance with the Remedies Law. Therefore, when a gambling contract is made as a result of deceit, when a betting contract is made under duress, or when an organizer of a lottery refuses to conduct it, the injured party has the right to rescind the contract.

611. Rescission in the Israeli legal system entails restitution: when a contract is rescinded, following the exercise of the right of rescission, each side is entitled to the restitution of what it has given under the contract. Therefore, in the above examples, the party rescinding a gambling, lottery or betting contract is entitled to the restitution of its money.

D. The Validity of the Contract

612. In contrast to section 30 which deals with invalid contracts, section 32(a) does not prescribe that gambling, lottery or betting contracts are void, but rather that such contracts are unenforceable. It appears that the gambling, lottery or betting contract governed by section 32(a) is a valid and effective contract. A number of arguments support this conclusion:

(1) Section 32(a) employs the word 'contract'. In other words, in order to fall within the ambit of this section, the existence of a contract made in accordance with the provisions of the first chapter of the General Contracts Law is required. For this reason, gambling, lotteries or betting agreements conducted only for the purpose of enjoyment and amusement are not included within section 32(a). These agreements lack intention to create a binding legal relation and in the absence of such intention no valid contract can be made under the Israeli legal system.
(2) Contracts within the scope of section 32(a) are devoid only of the rights to enforcement and damages. The validity of the contract can thus be inferred from the fact that the right of rescission is retained. It is not possible to rescind that which does not exist. The entire provision of section 32(a), denying certain remedies, applies only on the assumption that there exists a valid contract, since no remedies may be given for a void contract.
(3) When it is the intention of the legislator to establish the voidness of a particular contract it will normally be clearly expressed, as in the case of section 30 which establishes the rule in the case of invalid contracts.

613. The legal consequences of a gambling, lottery or betting contract may be inferred from its validity. The contract not only exists but also serves to effectuate obligatory results and the transfer of rights. Therefore, payment subject to such a contract remains in the possession of the receiver (unless there is ground for rescission, followed by restitution). However, a sum that has not yet been paid and to which one party is entitled by virtue of the contract cannot be claimed from the debtor. A gambling, lottery or betting contract creates a 'natural obligation' thus a person who receives money or property by virtue of this contract is a lawful possessor and will not be viewed as having obtained unlawful enrichment. A debtor who has paid his debt cannot be reimbursed since this payment was intended to pay off a 'natural debt'.

IV. Permitted Gambling, Lottery or Betting Contracts

614. The third category is that of permitted gambling, lottery or betting contracts. This category is based on section 32(b) of the General Contracts Law. Such contracts are both legal and enforceable.

615. Section 32(b) pertains to gambling, lottery or betting contracts 'regulated by law, or for which a permit for their conduct has been issued under any law'. These are essentially valid contracts, and section 32(b) expresses their restoration to the legitimate domains of the General Contracts Law and the Remedies Law.

616. Section 231 of the Penal Law is the criminal law parallel to section 32(b) of the General Contracts Law. This section serves to eliminate the element of criminality from the conduct of lotteries for which a permit has been granted in advance and from betting conducted by the (national) 'Payis Lottery Scheme' under permit. Section 231 of the Penal Law is consequently narrower and more specific than section 32(b) of the General Contracts Law. Therefore, lottery games which fall within the scope of the Penal Law will not be permissible, and any contract pertaining to these games will forever be illegal, falling into the purview of sections 30–31 of the General Contracts Law. The same is true in the case of lotteries and betting for which a permit has not been obtained under section 231. In the absence of a permit, these lotteries and betting are illegal and are subject to sections 30–31 of the General Contracts Law.

617. Section 32(b) distinguishes between gambling, lotteries or betting regulated by law and those for which a permit has been obtained under any law pertaining to their conduct. The first group includes betting regulated by the Sports Betting Regulations Law, 1967.[156] The latter comprises bets conducted by the National Lottery Scheme – 'Payis Lottery Scheme', as well as lotteries conducted by 'Magen David Adom' (the Israeli Red Cross) and the 'Soldier's Welfare Association' on accord of permits obtained and published occasionally in the official gazette. It is reasonable to assume that such permits are issued by the Minister of Finance in

156. 21 LSI 142.

accordance with public considerations, i.e., to non-profit organizations which promote public interests. There is also a social advantage gained in according permits for lotteries and betting; it serves to facilitate the natural impulse for gambling and channel it to regulated monitoring.

V. Contracts for Giving Marks or Grades

618. Section 33 of the General Contracts Law provides as follows:

> Where under any contract a mark, title, prize or the like is to be given according to a decision or evaluation by one of the parties or a third party, such decision or evaluation shall not be the subject of Court proceedings.

619. Section 33 deals with justiciability. The general rule of justiciability, according to which the court does not intervene in matters of policy, is usually applicable within constitutional law. However, it may also pertain to matters of private law, as illustrated by section 33. This section expresses the aversion to legal intervention in disputes that by nature are not subject to judicial determination.

620. Section 33 is based on the rule under which the court is not inclined to intervene in regard to issues which are subject to the discretion of professional experts. This rule may be implemented to all matters which are, by legal agreement or contractual provision, subject to the discretion, decision or determination of those who may be proficient in that field.

621. Section 33 may be divided into three parts:

(1) The type of contract in question: 'a contract under which a mark, a grade, title, prize or the like is to be given'.
(2) The test: 'according to a decision or evaluation by one of the parties or by a third party'.
(3) The results: 'that decision or evaluation will not be the subject of court proceedings'.

A. Definition

622. Here are a few examples of a contract under which a mark, title or prize will be awarded: a contract between a student and an academic institute awarding a grade or a degree; a contract for an athletic competition designating to award an Olympic title or a trophy, a contract for a contest intending to award the winner with a prize or with a medal. In contrast to section 32, which comprises a closed list of contracts, section 33 allows for an assortment of contracts ('or the like').

B. Decision or Evaluation

623. The test for decision or evaluation restricts the definition of the contract addressed by section 33. The section does not concern merely 'a contract under which a mark, a grade, title, prize or the like is to be given', but rather such a contract by which a mark, grade, title or prize will be awarded 'according to a decision or evaluation by of one of the parties or by a third party'. It is important to discern the distinction between 'decision' and 'evaluation'. A decision is a determination necessitating the choice between several possible outcomes and conducted according to clear objective criteria. In contrast, an evaluation is an approximate determination, being objective and less precise than a decision. For example, the determination regarding a winner in a race is a decision, while an ascertainment pertaining to the winner of a beauty contest or the award of a grade for an academic paper is an evaluation.

C. Results

624. A distinction must be made between the actual contract, for example, the contract between a student and the university, and the determination or evaluation made according to that contract, for example, the determination of the grade that the student is to receive in contract law. While the contract under which a mark, a grade, title, prize or the like is subject to legal claims, the determination or discretion pertaining to the mark, grade, title or prize, is not subject to court proceedings.

Chapter 4. Sale of Goods

§1. Introduction

625. The Sale Law, 1968, is one of the most important laws enacted in the wave of Israeli civil legislation. The sale is undoubtedly the most common transaction in the commercial world and in the daily life of virtually every person in modern society. The sale transaction may have various forms, and may take place in different circumstances.

626. The Sale Law is modelled along the lines of the Uniform Law of the International Sale of Goods, established and signed at the Hague Convention of July 1964. However, while the law incorporated the general principles, as well as some of the terms of the Uniform Law, it is not a duplicate thereof. First, the Sale Law applies to every sale and is not limited to international sales of goods. Second, the Sale Law is a general law, applying not only to the sale of goods but also to the sale of land, rights and exchange.

627. The Sale Law was enacted in order to serve as a specific law, dealing with the particular aspects of a sale. In contrast, the general aspects regarding the creation and breach of an agreement and provisions concerning general aspects of the relationship between contractual parties are addressed within the general laws of contracts, pursuant to the provisions of the General Contracts Law and the Remedies Law. As a result, the provisions of the Uniform Law were modified and adapted to the specific nature of the Sale Law. However, the provisions of the Uniform Law were fully incorporated in the Sale Law (International Sale of Goods), 1971, which applies exclusively to the international sale of goods.

628. While the Sale Law should primarily be viewed as a specific law – resulting in the provisions of the general laws of contracts applying to sale agreements only when there is no specific provision in the Sale Law – the Sale Law is also a general law, applying to different types of sale transactions. By the same token, other more specific laws may contain particular provisions concerning specific types of sale transactions which will thus take precedence over the relatively more general provisions of the Sale Law (e.g., pursuant to section 8 of the Land Law, 1969, the sale of land requires written agreement). The provisions of the Sale Law shall apply where no contrary intention appears from the agreement between the parties.

§2. The Nature of Sale

629. A sale is defined in section 1 of the Sale Law as 'a transfer of the ownership of property for a price'. Hence, the law defines sale in terms of a 'real' transaction, emphasizing the element of the transfer of ownership. However, the law does not disregard the obligatory aspects of the sale. In fact, it is apparent from the entire structure of the law's provisions, as well as certain explicit provisions, that the law also deals with future sales and future agreements to sell property. This wide interpretation of the law is necessary in order to accommodate the law to the requirements or demands of the commercial world. A 'real' transaction, in which the consideration is paid and the property and the ownership right therein are immediately transferred to the buyer, is indeed a common occurrence in everyday life. However, more complex transactions, in which the ownership and possession of the property are transferred at a time subsequent to the creation of the agreement (e.g., the commodities exchange), are prevalent features of the modern commercial world.

630. The transfer of ownership rights in the property and not any other lesser right is the element that distinguishes the sale from other transactions. Such rights entitle the owner to full control over the property and enable him to enjoy all the financial advantages related to ownership. Other laws, dealing with various kinds of transactions, concern only rights which derive from ownership such as pledge or hire. All such rights entitle their possessor to fewer advantages than those which may be derived from actual ownership of the property. Accordingly, a transaction may only be defined as a sale if it involves the transfer of ownership rights.

631. The sale must be made for consideration. The transfer of ownership, otherwise than for consideration, will be deemed a gift. However, consideration does not have to transpire in money, and the Sale Law applies also to exchanges. The requirement of consideration constitutes an exception to the general rule of Israeli contract law according to which consideration is not required for the formation of a valid contract. Section 2 determines 'the main materials test' in order to differentiate between a sales transaction and a contract for services. If the party manufacturing or producing the property supplied its main materials, the contract is perceived as a contract of sale. However, if the party that orders the property undertakes to provide its main materials, the contract is a contract for services, and the provisions of the Contract for Services Law, 1974, will apply.[157]

632. The Sale Law imposes two main obligations on the parties: pursuant to section 7, the seller must deliver the object sold to the buyer and transfer the ownership to him (hereinafter: the duty of delivery and transfer). The buyer, pursuant to section 19, must pay the purchase price to the seller and take delivery of the object sold (hereinafter: the duty to pay and take delivery). The seller's duty to deliver the object sold and the buyer's duty to pay its price are concurrent obligations, to be fulfilled simultaneously. Accordingly, failure of one of the parties to perform its obligation allows the other party to withhold its corresponding obligation. Hence, completion of the transaction is dependent on both parties.

633. The time frame in which the seller performs his obligation and delivers the object sold to the buyer is of primary importance. Unless the parties have otherwise agreed, it is at this point in time that ownership in the object sold transfers to the buyer. The delivery of the object sold then modifies the status of the parties *inter se*,

---

157. For further discussion of the Contract for Services Law, *see* paras 650–655.

the buyer becoming the owner of the object sold and the seller receiving the purchase price. At that point, the transaction is completed, and the parties are under no further obligations, unless agreed otherwise.

634. Delivery is also the point in time at which the risk passes from seller to buyer. As long as the ownership right and the control over the object sold remain in the hands of the seller, the risk for any loss or damage to the object sold is borne by the seller. Hence, where the object sold is lost or devaluates before the buyer has delivered it, the buyer is relieved of his obligations, and the seller will not be entitled to demand fulfilment by the buyer of the buyer's obligations under the contract. After delivery, the seller is entitled to receive the purchase price and any loss to the object sold will be under the responsibility of the buyer.

635. In order to ensure that the buyer acquires full ownership rights of the object sold and that his rights will not be subordinate to other pre-existing rights, the seller must deliver the object sold free of every charge, commitment or other third-party rights. Moreover, the seller must immediately give notice to the buyer of any claim of a third-party right in respect of the object sold as he knew of, or ought to have known of before delivery.

636. If the buyer bought the property in the conditions of market overt (i.e., chattels sold by a person who carries on the sale of property of the kind of the object sold, the sale being made in the ordinary course of business) he will receive the ownership free of every charge, attachment, seizure or other right in the object sold. The same applies even if the seller is not the owner thereof, or he is not entitled to transfer it as previously mentioned, provided that the buyer buys and takes possession of it in good faith. The concept of market overt allows the buyer to receive the full property right in the object sold. Any claim or right, which a third party may have against the seller in relation to the object sold, will be converted to the price received for it.

§3. The Obligations of the Seller

637. The primary duty of the seller is to deliver the object sold to the buyer and consequently to transfer to him the ownership therein. The delivery is made by placing the object sold at the disposal of the buyer (section 8(a)) or placing it at the disposal of a carrier, where its carriage has been agreed upon, provided that the carrier is liable to the buyer under the contract of carriage. In effect, any action which enables the buyer to receive the object sold will be deemed delivery; hence, the meaning of the term 'delivery' will vary in accordance with the nature of the object sold (i.e., chattels, land or rights). The law provides that the date of delivery shall be within reasonable time after the conclusion of the contract or within the period that has been agreed upon and after reasonable advance notice. The place of delivery shall be at the seller's place of business or the seller's place of residence.

638. The seller is under an obligation to deliver the object sold in accordance with the details agreed upon between the parties. The defects described below will be considered as non-conformity, and the delivery of non-conforming property will be considered a breach of contract. The seller will not be considered to have fulfilled his obligations if he has delivered:

(1) Only a part of the object sold or a quantity greater or smaller than that agreed upon.
(2) Different property or property of a different kind or description from that agreed upon.
(3) Property lacking the quality or characteristics necessary for its ordinary or commercial use or for a particular purpose appearing from the agreement.
(4) Property which in respect of its kind, description, quality or characteristics does not conform to the model or sample which was shown to the buyer, unless it was shown without responsibility being assumed for conformity.
(5) Property which in some other respect does not conform to what has been agreed upon between the parties.

639. The rationale for the above provisions is clear: while the object sold is not delivered to the buyer, the seller has full control thereof and is (or should be) aware of any defect or non-conformity of the property. Hence, the seller's failure to notify the buyer of such defects or non-conformity of the property, and the delivery of such property to the buyer – contrary to his expectations – may be considered, on the part of the seller, as conduct which infringes his duty to act in good faith.

640. However, the buyer will be entitled to rely on the provisions concerning non-conformity if he knew of the non-conformity at the time of the conclusion of the contract. In such case, the buyer will be deemed to have had agreed upon buying the non-conforming property.

641. While the buyer is required to examine the object sold immediately after receipt thereof, the seller is required to give the buyer, upon his demand, a suitable opportunity to examine the object sold before the receipt thereof. The buyer is required to give the seller notice of any non-conformity immediately after the time of the examination, or immediately after discovering the non-conformity, whichever is earlier. If the buyer does not give notice of the non-conformity, he or she shall not be entitled to rely on it. In the notice of non-conformity, the buyer shall specify the non-conformity in reasonable detail and shall give the seller a suitable opportunity to examine the object sold.

642. Again, the rationale for the above provisions is clear: a reasonable buyer who upon receiving control over the object sold and examining it as required, discovers any defects or non-conformity, will immediately demand the remedies for non-conformity. These remedies might require the repair or rescission of the agreement. Therefore, if the buyer fails to do so, he will be deemed to have waived his rights and to have accepted the property in its condition upon delivery.

643. The duty of notice is also required in order to differentiate between non-conformity which existed before delivery and damage caused to the property after delivery to the buyer. While the former is under the responsibility of the seller, the latter is not.

644. Where the non-conformity could not have been discovered by a reasonable examination at the time of delivery (i.e., in the case of latent non-conformity), the buyer shall be entitled to rely on it, provided that he gives notice to the seller immediately upon actually discovering it. However, the rights of the buyer in this respect are restricted: in the case of a sale of chattels the buyer shall not be entitled to rescind the contract if he gave notice more than two years after delivery of the object sold, and he shall not be entitled to the other remedies for breach of contract if he gave notice more than four years after delivery. Notwithstanding these restrictions or those of any agreement, where the non-conformity arises out of facts which the seller knew or ought to have known at the time the contract was concluded, and which he did not disclose to the buyer, the buyer shall be entitled to rely on the non-conformity. However, this is true only as long as the buyer gives notice of it to the seller immediately upon preservation of the buyer's rights to remedies for non-conformity.

§4. The Obligations of the Buyer

645. The buyer has one primary duty: to pay the price for the object sold. The law provides that a proper price shall be paid, unless the parties have agreed otherwise. Payment shall be made on the date of delivery at the seller's place of business or residence.

646. The buyer is also required to take delivery of the object sold, and to examine it. The taking of the delivery and examination are important in order to allow the seller to fulfil all his obligations and to complete the transaction.

§5. Remedies

647. Both parties are entitled to all the remedies provided under the Remedies Law, as well as to the specific remedies established under the Sale Law.

648. One such specific remedy involves the reduction of the purchase price. If the seller fails to deliver property conforming to the contract, the buyer shall be entitled to deduct from the price the amount by which the value of the object sold has decreased in consequence of the non-conformity as compared with its value according to the contract.

649. Where the buyer has been given the right to determine any particular relating to the object sold or to the terms of the sale and fails to do so within the time agreed upon in the contract, the seller shall be entitled to determine that particular himself, having regard to the buyer's requirements as far as they are known to him.

Chapter 5. Contract for Services (Building Contracts)

§1. Introduction

650. A contract for services is a contract for the performance of any work, or the rendering of any service, for remuneration, where the contractor is not an employee of the customer.

§2. Obligations of the Parties

651. A contract for service is regulated by the Contract for Services Law, 1974. However, a contract for the supply of property to be produced or manufactured where the contractor undertakes to provide the main part of the materials necessary therefore is governed by the Sale Law, 1968. According to the Contract for Services Law the contractor is bound to do the work or render the service, while the customer is bound to pay the agreed remuneration.

§3. Remedies for Defect

652. Where the work or service is not in conformity with that agreed upon, the customer must notify the contractor of the defect within reasonable time after he discovered or should have discovered it, and if the defect can be repaired, must give the contractor a suitable opportunity to repair it.

653. If the contractor does not repair the defect within reasonable time after the customer acted as provided above, the customer may rectify the defect and claim reimbursement of his reasonable expenses from the contractor, or so long as the defect has not been repaired, deduct the amount by which in consequence of the defect, the value of work or service is less than the agreed amount of remuneration.

§4. Lien

654. The contractor has a lien on any property delivered to him by the customer for the performance of the work or the rendering of the service, against the amount due to him from the customer in consequence of the transaction.

§5. PASSING OF RISK

655. Where the work or service is performed on property in the possession of the contractor, the customer shall take delivery of such property at the time agreed upon or, in the absence of agreement, within reasonable time after the contractor notifies him that he has completed the work or service. The customer shall be released from the obligation to pay the remuneration unless the property is lost or damaged after the customer should have taken delivery and from a cause for which the contractor is not responsible.

Chapter 6. Hire and Loan

§1. Introduction

656. The various provisions of hire, lease and loan contracts are governed in the Israeli legal system by the provisions of the Hire and Loan Law, 1971. This law replaced the previous provisions concerning such contracts, which were based on the Ottoman Mejelle and the Common Law.

§2. Basic Principles

657. The Hire and Loan Law perceives the relations between the parties as contractual and obligatory, in divergence to common law, which classifies these relations as part of property law.

658. In resemblance to any other contract, hire contracts are created by an agreement between the parties. Consequently, hire agreements are regulated by the General Contracts Law together with the provisions of the Hire and Loan Law. Thus, for example, the Hire and Loan Law determines a particular form for termination of the contract which is different to the forms for termination stipulated in the General Contracts Law. The general principle of freedom of contract also governs the hire agreement, as provided in section 2(c) of the Hire and Loan Law: 'The provisions of this chapter shall apply where no other law contains special provisions as to the matter in question and no contrary intention appears from the agreement between the parties.' Except for two provisions (sections 8 and 22, which deal with the exemption of the lessor for non-conformity or defect and the transfer of hire) the parties to the agreement may choose to deviate from the provisions of the law.

659. Besides the provisions of the Hire and Loan Law and the General Contracts Law, the hire agreement is also governed by specific provisions addressing hire in other laws, such as the Land Law 1969, concerning with land tenancy; the Protection of Tenant Law 1972, concerning with statutory tenancy and applying special provisions during the period of the hire agreement and thereafter in special circumstances and the Bailment Law 1967, addressing special aspects of the possession of property.

660. The hire laws also give rise to property rights which are vested in both parties. The law deals with certain aspects of these rights, in conjunction with the Land Law 1971 and the Movable Property Law, 1971. Initially the lessor has an ownership right in his property (the hired property) and although he transfers the possession and use to the lesser he still enjoys certain rights derived from his ownership. Moreover, the lessee's rights in the hired property are subordinate to the lessor's ownership rights. Thus the lessee is unable to transfer his rights or sublet the hired property without the consent of the lessor and upon termination of the hire the hired property returns to the full possession and use of the lessor. The rights of the lessee are also, in some respects, property rights. During the period of hire he has the right to possess and use the hired property, a right which is protected in rem.

661. A further principle of the Hire and Loan Law is the equal consideration awarded to the interests of both parties. The lessor's rights in his property are protected, as are the interests of the lessee concerning enjoyment derived of his possession and use of the hired property.

662. The Hire and Loan Law is a general law, which concerns all kinds of property, including land, personal property and rights.

§3. The Nature of Hire

663. According to section 1 of the Hire and Loan Law '(a) hire is a right conferred for consideration ... to possess and use property, otherwise than permanently'. During the period of hire, the lessor transfers part of his property rights – the possession and use in the hired property – to the lessee, while maintaining his ownership of them. Accordingly, during the period of hire, the lessee may enjoy the use and the possession of the property, and the lessor has a duty to allow him complete and undisturbed use of the hired property. The hire subordinates the contracting parties to a set of correlating rights and duties.

664. The hire contract must be made with consideration. A right to possess and use property otherwise than permanently, conferred without consideration, is a loan. Some of the provisions of the law are also applied to the loan (Chapter 2 of the law). In the case where the contracting parties resolved that consideration would be paid, but did not agree regarding the exact sum, the rent to be paid is the rent which would have been appropriate at the time of the formation of the contract. The right of the lessor to receive the rent is a contractual right and as such is subject to the general laws of obligation (the rent may be transferred to another according to the Transfer of Obligations Law 1969).

665. The period of hire commences at the time agreed upon in the contract or, in the absence of agreement, when the item hired is delivered to the lessee. The period of hire may not be permanent, although it may be unlimited or for a lengthy period of time. If the parties did not agree upon the date of the termination each party may terminate the hire by giving notice to the other party.

666. The rights of the lessor and of the lessee are transferrable to third parties. The lessor may confer his rights in the item hired to another person. The rights of the new lessor in that which has been hired are subordinate to the rights of the lessee to it. As long as the lessee does not know about the transfer of the ownership in the item hired he is exempt from fulfilling his duties to the new lessor.

667. The lessee may also transfer his rights or sublet the item hired to another lessee, but he must do so with the consent of the lessor. The lessor is entitled to choose the persons allowed to possess and use his property, but any objection on his part to the transfer of the lessee's rights, or to the subletting, must be based on reasonable grounds. The lessor can also stipulate conditions to his consent, but such conditions must be reasonable. If the lessor objects to the transfer of the lessee's rights or to the subletting on unreasonable grounds, the lessee is entitled to effect the transaction of real estate without the consent of the lessor. This is also true when the lessor stipulates unreasonable conditions to his consent in the case where no reservation has been stipulated in the contract. If such reservation has been specified in a real estate lease agreement, the matter is left to the court's discretion to determine whether the lessor's objection is reasonable. However, if the lease pertains to chattels, the court may give effect to the transaction subject to certain conditions it deems as appropriate.

§4. The Duties of the Lessor

668. During the period of hire the lessor has a property right (ownership) in the hired property, while the lessee is allowed to possess and use it. This distribution of property rights among the contracting parties subordinates each of them to a correlating set of rights and duties, intended to protect the ownership rights of the lessor and to enable the lessee to have complete and undisturbed use of his possession in the hired property.

669. The first duty of the lessor is to deliver that which has been hired to the lessee and to place it at his disposal. The delivery shall take place at the time agreed upon in the contract. If the time of the delivery was not agreed upon, the delivery shall take place within reasonable time after the formation of the contract following reasonable notice. The lessor is also under a duty to deliver the hired property vacant; otherwise the lessee will not be able to take possession thereof. Failure to deliver the hired property shall be considered a breach of contract.

670. Moreover, the lessor shall not be considered to have fulfilled his obligations if 'he has delivered to the lessee property which at the time of the delivery did not, in respect of its kind, description quality or characteristics or otherwise, conform to what has been agreed between the parties' (section 6). The purpose of this provision is quite clear: the owner of the hired property (the lessor) is usually aware of its defects before it is delivered to the lessee, thus his duty is to disclose any relevant information pertaining to his possession, to the lessee, before the formation of the contract. Failure to do so constitutes a breach of contract. However, not every non-conformity shall constitute a breach of contract. Pursuant to section 6, the lessee is not entitled to rely on non-conformity if he knew of it at the time of the formation of the contract.

671. The definition of non-conformity is broad enough to encompass a large variety of defects which may have existed in that which has been hired before its delivery to the lessee. The residuary term 'otherwise' in the definition of non-conformity in section 6 (cited above) tends to increase the number of possible situations giving rise to non-conformity. Thus, even non-conformity in the surroundings of the thing hired shall be considered as non-conformity.

672. The hire may be regarded as a set of continuous contractual relations. This fact, together with the considerable weight attributed to the lessee's rights to use that which has been hired, leads to the imposition of duties on the lessor during the period of hire, especially the duty to repair defects in the thing that has been hired and to refrain from any disturbance to the lessee impairing his complete and undisturbed use.

673. The primary duty of the lessor is to repair defects in the thing that has been hired.

Section 7 provides as follows:

> The lessor shall, within a reasonable time after receiving a demand to this effect from the lessee, repair any such defect in the thing hired, or in any property in his possession serving the thing hired, as defeats or substantially limits the use of the thing hired according to the agreement or according to what is customary in the circumstances (such a defect hereinafter referred to as 'defect'), whether the defect existed at the time the thing hired was delivered to the lessee or came into existence thereafter.

674. This duty covers various defects in the hired property or in any other property in the possession of the lessor serving it. This may include the surroundings of the hired property – as the yard, the rooftop or the stairway to the hired flat – which are in the co-possession of a number of tenants including the lessee. The lessor is under a duty to repair the hired property within reasonable time, and failure to do so shall constitute a breach of contract entitling the lessee to certain remedies.

675. The duty of the lessor to repair defects in the hired property prevails during the entire period of the hire, and derives from the right of the lessee to enjoyment of the hired property during the period of the hire, as agreed upon or as customary in the circumstances of the case.

676. Section 7 provides certain exceptions to the duty of the lessor to repair the hired property and imposes it upon the lessee. First, the agreement between the parties may exempt the lessor from this duty. However, not every exemption is permitted by law. In accordance with section 8, if the lessor knew or ought to have known of the non-conformity at the time of the formation of the contract and he did not disclose such facts to the lessee, the lessee will still be entitled to his rights under sections 6 and 7, notwithstanding the agreement between the parties. The lessor may also be exempt from liability for defects pursuant to the Bailees Law, 1967. According to section 2(b) of the Bailees Law, expressly incorporated into the Hire and Loan Law, the lessee should be regarded as responsible for any damage to the hired property, which occurred while in his possession, unless he can prove that the damage did not occur as a result of his negligence. According to section 2(d) of the Bailees Law the lessee is also responsible for any damage that could have been avoided had he given the lessor proper notice thereof. The lessor is also exempt from repairing a defect which is customarily within the duty of the lessee to repair.

677. A final exemption from the lessor's duty to repair is provided in section 10, which deals with extreme circumstances where the defect is a:

> result of circumstances which at the time of the making of the contract the lessor did not know of or foresee and need not have known of or foreseen and which he could have obviated, and its repair under these circumstances is impossible or would impose on the lessor an obligation fundamentally different from what has been agreed.

678. A further important duty of the lessor is provided in section 11:

> The lessor shall enable the lessee to use the thing hired, during the period of hire, in accordance with what has been agreed between the parties without interference by him or on his behalf.

679. As previously stated, the primary interest of the lessee in the hire is the use of that which has been hired. Hence, the lessor is under the correlating duty to enable the lessee to enjoy complete and undisturbed use in the hired property, either by repairing the defects or by refraining from any action or harassment which may disturb the enjoyment of the lessee in it, as agreed between the parties. This duty is considered part of the hire agreement, and part of the lessor's general duty to perform the agreement in good faith (section 4 of the Hire and Loan Law and section 39 of the General Contracts Law). Failure to fulfil this duty constitutes a breach of contract and entitles the lessee to claim remedies in tort law and in property law.

§5. The Duties of the Lessee

680. The lessee is under an obligation to take possession of the thing hired immediately upon its delivery by the lessor.

681. The primary duty imposed on the lessee during the period of hire is to pay rent to the lessor. The rent constitutes consideration for the lessee's right to possess the hired property. If the parties agreed that rent shall be paid, but did not specify the amount or the manner of its determination, the rent paid shall be in accordance with the proper rate at the time of the formation of the contract.

682. However, since the rent constitutes consideration for the right to possess and use the hired property, the lessee may be exempt from payment or part thereof, in certain circumstances, as when the possession or the quiet use of the lessee in the hired property is in some way defective or diminished, either as a result of the behaviour of the lessor or as a result of unforeseen circumstances. In such cases the lessee will be exempt from the duty to pay the rent as a remedy for the lessor's breach of contract, or as a remedy for the frustration of the contract.

683. The first exemption from the payment of rent, in circumstances constituting a breach of contract on the part of the lessor, is governed by the provisions of section 9(2), which addresses remedies for the lessor's failure to repair defects in the hired property, as required under section 7. In such cases, so long as the defect in the hired property has not been repaired, the lessee is entitled to reduce the rent in proportion to the decrease in the value of the hire, in consequence of the unrepaired defect. This provision has two purposes: first, to provide the lessee with some means to exert pressure on the lessor to repair the defect in the hired property and second, to indemnify the lessee for the unexpected reduction in the value of his possession and use of the hired property.

684. A further remedy available to the lessee on account of the lessor's failure to repair the defect in the hired property is to repair the defect himself and then demand that the lessor reimburse his reasonable expenses. However, if the lessee wishes to repair the hired property, even though the lessor is responsible for the repair, he must give the lessor reasonable advance notice in writing. If the repair of the hired property is urgent, in effect that the lessee cannot be expected to wait for the lessor to repair the defect, the lessee may repair the defect without giving such proper advance notice to the lessor. The lessee will then be entitled to demand that the lessor reimburse his reasonable expenses.

685. Section 15(a), addressing circumstances of the frustration of hire, provides as follows:

> Where the thing hired is immovable property and the lessee is precluded from using it for the purpose of the hire by circumstances connected with the thing hired or with the means of access there and he does not rescind the contract on that account, he shall be exempt from paying rent for the period during which use it precluded.

686. This exemption from payment of the rent is given to the lessee if, at the time of formation of the contract, the lessee did not know of or foresee, and could not have known or foreseen, the circumstances described in section 15, and could not have avoided them.

687. Given the duty of the lessor to enable the lessee to use the thing hired in the agreed manner, the circumstances described in section 15 will be considered a breach of contract entitling the lessee various remedies. The lessee may, under such circumstances, rescind the contract. Alternatively, he may exercise his rights under section 15 and withhold payment of rent. However, the exemption provided in section 15 is only a temporary one. Once the circumstances impairing the lessee's use in the thing hired are rectified, the lessee must continue to pay the rent. Section 15, then, provides a mechanism whereby the lessee, faced with frustrating circumstances of a temporary nature, will not be forced to rescind the contract.

688. Section 16 of the Hire and Loan Law addressing the proper use of the thing hired provides as follows:

> The lessee shall not use the thing hired save as agreed; provided that if such use has not been stipulated as the sole use he may use the thing hired for some other use so long as this does not involve damage to the thing hired or burden the lessor more heavily than agreed.

689. The right of the lessee to use the thing hired is, therefore, subordinate to the provisions of the agreement between the parties. If the agreement determined the exclusive use designated to the lessee, the lessee may not use the thing hired for any other purpose without the consent of the lessor, with the exception of minor usage incidental to the exclusive use agreed upon. If the proper interpretation of the agreement indicates that certain allowed employment of the hired property, prescribed in the agreement, are not determined as exclusive uses, then the lessee will be entitled under section 16 to any use which does not damage the thing hired or does not impose a heavy burden on the lessor. If the agreement did not prescribe any allowed use in the thing hired, then the use in the thing hired shall be as customary, according to the nature of the thing hired and the identity of the parties.

690. Damage to the hired goods, or heavy burden on the lessor, does not have to actually occur before the lessor will be entitled to prohibit the lessee's use. It is sufficient that the lessor be under reasonable apprehension that the use not agreed upon will cause damage to the hired goods, or lay a heavy burden upon it. Such damage may be to the intactness of the hired goods, or to their economic value. Furthermore, the lessor will be entitled to prohibit usage not agreed upon if such usage will lead to a breach of the lessor's duties towards a third party (e.g., establishing a business in a private building, where the lessor has promised the other tenants that the hired property shall be used for habitation purposes only). If the lessee uses the hired goods in a manner not agreed upon which does not fall within the circumstances described in section 16, such unauthorized usage shall be considered a breach of contract.

691. A further duty of the lessee, related to the lessee's proper use of the hired goods, is provided in section 17, which provides as follows:

> The lessee shall at any reasonable time enable the lessor to inspect the thing hired and carry out repairs thereon, provided that the lessor gives him reasonable advance notice and disturbs him as little as possible.

692. The lessor has a legitimate economic interest in safeguarding the intactness of the hired goods and in ensuring it remains in good condition during the entire period of the hire. These interests are protected under section 17. Obviously, the lessor will not be able to safeguard his interests in the hired goods without the cooperation of the lessee, who has actual physical possession of it. Hence, the lessee is required by law to allow the lessor to inspect the hired goods so as to ensure that it is being maintained in reasonable condition.

693. The lessee in under an obligation to return the hired goods to the possession and use of the lessor upon the termination of hire. If the hired goods are property, they shall be returned vacant. The termination of the period of hire will be as agreed upon in the contract. If the period of hire has not been agreed upon, or if the parties extend the period agreed upon, without stipulating a new one, each party may terminate the hire by giving notice to the other party. The lessee must return the hired goods to the lessor in a condition which will allow the lessor to take possession of them. Hence, it should be vacant from the lessee's belongings and unoccupied by third parties. The lessee must also return the hired goods in good condition and repair any damages which occurred during the period of hire, for which the lessee is responsible under section 7. The expectation is that the lessee will return the hired goods in the same condition in which he received them, save for ordinary wear and tear.

Chapter 7. Compromise Settlement

§1. Introduction

694. A compromise settlement is a special kind of a contract, in which parties agree to terminate a dispute that arose, or might arise between them, by mutually waiving contractual or legal rights. Such a contract can be approved by the court, whereby the contract becomes part of a judgment.

§2. The Nature of a Compromise Settlement

695. A compromise settlement approved by the court creates a double bond. It binds the contracting parties as a contract, while at the same time it creates a res judicata between those parties. Therefore, a compromise settlement combines attributes of a contract and a judgment. Constituting a contract, a compromise settlement can be annulled or repealed like any other contract. Thus, for example, a compromise settlement that was formulated by misrepresentation is voidable, according to section 15 of the General Contracts Law. By the same token, an illegal compromise is void, according to section 30 of the General Contracts Law. A compromise approved by the court can be annulled only in accordance with the procedures for modifying or repealing legal judgments.

§3. Legal Policy

696. The legal policy in Israel is to encourage and approve settlements and compromises. As long as the compromise is based on the free will of the parties, the courts will not intervene in its contents.

Chapter 8. Guarantee

§1. Introduction

697. The guarantee involves a special relationship between three different parties: the creditor, the debtor and the guarantor. The Guarantee Law, 1967, is one of the various specific contract laws, enacted by the Israeli legislator over the last five decades. Following the established pattern, it is concise, based on the principles of the General Contracts Law, especially the provisions concerning situations involving several debtors and creditors, as applied to the special set of relationships which exist between the creditor, the debtor and the guarantor. The Guarantee Law is a dispositive law, which is thus applicable when no contrary intention appears from the agreement between the parties.

§2. The Nature of the Guarantee

698. Section 1 of the Guarantee Law defines the guarantee as 'a person's undertaking to fulfil another person's obligation towards a third person'.

699. Hence the guarantee involves a triple set of relationships: the relationship between the debtor and the creditor, the relationship between the creditor and the guarantor and the relationship between the debtor and the guarantor. The relationship between the debtor and the creditor creates the guaranteed obligation; the relationship between the creditor and the guarantor creates the creditor's right to demand fulfilment of the guaranteed obligation from the guarantor where the debtor has failed to fulfil his obligation; and finally, the relationship between the debtor and the guarantor gives the guarantor the right to resort to the debtor and to be reimbursed for what he has paid in fulfilling his guarantee.

700. The second and third sets of the above relationships are governed by the provisions of the Guarantee Law. The guarantee is created by agreement between the guarantor and the creditor or by an undertaking of the guarantor of which notice has been given to the creditor. No formal requirements are needed to create a valid guarantee. The guarantee may be made either orally or in writing and may stipulate any terms agreed upon between the parties. The formulation of the agreement or the notification thereof, establishes both the relationship between the creditor and the guarantor, as well as the one between the guarantor and the debtor. The relationship between the debtor and the creditor is dealt with by the general laws of contract.

701. The guarantee is a dependent obligation. Its validity is derived not only from the agreement between the creditor and the guarantor, but also from the validity of the agreement between the debtor and the creditor. The primary purpose of the guarantee agreement is not to create an independent obligation, but rather to establish means of assisting the creditor with respect to the fulfilment of the primary obligations in the case of default by the debtor. Hence, performance of the guarantee is normally claimed only if the debtor has failed to comply with the guaranteed obligation.

702. The accessory nature of the guarantee has numerous implications concerning the applicable legal rules. First, the guarantee can relate only to a valid obligation. If the guaranteed obligation is itself void, the guarantor will be discharged from his obligation. Moreover, any plea the debtor may have against the creditor in relation to the guaranteed obligation is extended to the guarantor. Hence, where the claim against the debtor becomes prescribed, the claim against the guarantor also becomes prescribed, assuming it has not been claimed beforehand. A second implication of the accessory nature of the guarantee is the correspondence in scope between the guarantor's obligation and that of the debtor. The scope of the guarantor's liability to the obligation cannot exceed the debtor's, nor should the obligation be more onerous. However, unless contrary intention materializes, the guarantor will be liable for any interest, expenses and damages payable by the debtor in respect of the guaranteed obligation, and all of these shall be regarded in the same way as the guaranteed obligation itself. Where, however, the extent of the guarantee is restricted, the guarantor will not be liable beyond the scope of his guarantee.

§3. The Relationship Between the Creditor and the Guarantor

703. The first set of relationships considered in the Guarantee Law is between the creditor and the guarantor. The guarantor undertakes to fulfil the debtor's obligation towards the creditor. The guarantee may relate to the obligation as a whole, or may pertain to part of an existing or future, revolving or conditional, liquidated or unliquidated obligation. The only limitation on the terms and scope of the guarantee derive, as explained above, from the nature of the guarantee as an obligation accessory to the debtor's obligation.

704. Where the guaranteed obligation is reduced, by agreement between the debtor and the creditor or by waiver of the creditor, the guarantor is discharged to the same extent as the debtor. Otherwise, the guarantor's obligation would, in effect, attain an existence independent from that of the debtors. However, where the guaranteed obligation is increased, by agreement between the debtor and the creditor, the obligation of the guarantor is not affected thereby. This provision is essential in order to protect the rights of the guarantor and to prevent a situation in which the creditor and the debtor will be able to affect the liability of the guarantor by an agreement between them, without obtaining the guarantor's consent. Where any other variation occurs in the guaranteed obligation by agreement between the debtor and the creditor, the obligation of the guarantor is modified respectively, provided that the guarantor shall have an option to fulfil his guarantee without variation if it is possible to do so, or to rescind the guarantee if the variation is a basic variation which detriments the rights of the guarantor.

705. The guarantee is a conditional obligation: the guarantor will be required to fulfil the guarantee only if the debtor fails to fulfil the terms of the guaranteed obligation. Moreover, as stated above, the creditor may not request fulfilment of the guarantee from the guarantor without having first requested fulfilment of the obligation from the debtor. The guarantor may, however, waive this right. Furthermore, the creditor will be entitled to resort to the guarantor before requesting fulfilment from the debtor, if the debtor is under a receiving order or a winding-up order or if the debtor has died, is abroad or if the request involves special difficulties.

706. The creditor must refrain from causing damage to the guarantor. Hence, where the creditor had caused the non-fulfilment of the guaranteed obligation, the guarantor will be discharged. Furthermore, where the creditor had caused the termination of a security given to secure the guaranteed obligation, and damage is thereby caused to the guarantor, the guarantor will be discharged to the amount of the damage.

§4. The Relationship Between the Debtor and the Guarantor

707. As stated above, the guarantor and the debtor are jointly and severally liable to the creditor. The primary right of the guarantor is to resort to the debtor and be recouped by him for what the guarantor has paid in fulfilling his guarantee, in addition to reasonable expenses incurred by him in consequence of the guarantee and interest. Hence, ultimately the burden of the debt will continue to rest upon the debtor. However, the guarantor may not resort to the debtor if the guarantee has been given without the debtor's consent. This exception to the general rule is important in view of the fact that the guarantee might be created by an agreement between the creditor and the guarantor without the approval of the debtor. Such an agreement will not bind the debtor (a third party) unless the debtor has agreed to the creation of the guarantee.

708. The accessory nature of guarantee is reflected in the rule of the Guarantee Law according to which any plea a debtor may have against the creditor in relation to the obligation shall also be available to the guarantor. Because the duties of the guarantor are derived from those of the debtor, any plea which may reduce or rescind the debtor's duties must necessarily affect the guarantor's duties. In order to protect the interests of the debtor, the law provides that the guarantor shall not be entitled to resort to the debtor as long as the latter might have been discharged from paying his debt to the creditor. This is true as long as the debtor has a claim against the creditor, and that the guarantor – albeit knowing of this claim – did not use it to protect himself. Therefore, if the guarantor does not exercise due care and neglects his defence, thereby causing harm to the interests of the debtor, he may not resort to the debtor. These provisions shall not apply if the guarantor fulfilled his guarantee after sending the debtor notice of his intention to do so and giving him reasonable time to apply to the court. This notification awards the debtor some degree of control over the payment of the debt and the opportunity to ensure that any rights he may have against the creditor are given practical effect.

709. After the fulfilment of the guarantee, the guarantor will, in effect, step into the shoes of the creditor as regards the latter's rights against the debtor and the remedies which the creditor was entitled to. Hence, where the guaranteed obligation is also secured by a charge on property of the debtor, the charge shall, after fulfilment of the guarantee, be conferred to the guarantor in order to secure his right to resort to the debtor.

§5. The Guarantee Law (Amendment), 1992

710. In 1992 the Guarantee Law was amended in respect of guarantees of individual guarantors. The amendment applies only to guarantees for loans, which are intended for the purchase of apartments or loans for a certain maximum amount, that changes periodically. The purpose of the amendment is to protect individual guarantors that had previously been innocent victims of the sophisticated banks. The provisions of the amendment are now *ius cogens* and cannot be altered in any contract, save for the benefit of an individual guarantor.

711. The main provisions of the amendment are as follows:

(1) Prior to taking any legal action towards an individual guarantor, all legal means against the debtor must be exhausted, including judgment and execution proceedings.
(2) Several guarantors are liable in equal and proportional shares.
(3) Guarantees must be in specified amounts.

§6. The Guarantee Law (Amendment), 1997

712. In 1997 the Guarantee Law was re-amended. The amendment served to balance between the rights of the guarantor to those of the creditor. On the one hand, it narrows the definition of a creditor and provides a broader protection to the guarantor, including an extensive duty of disclosure imposed on the creditor. On the other hand, it narrows the definition of an individual guarantor and excludes corporations from its definition, thus increasing the course of action available to the creditor in collecting his debt. It also increases the amount of the guarantee given and thus effectively reduces eligibility for Chapter 2 of the Guarantee Law.

Chapter 9. Pledge

§1. Introduction

713. The Pledges Law, 1967, replaces the previous law of pledges that was based on the Mejelle and on the common law. The institution of pledge is of great importance in Israeli commercial and economic life. Loans, bank accounts and bonds are secured by charges on property which constitute a primary source for the collection of unpaid debts. Accordingly, the Pledges Law has similar importance, being the legal tool for the creation of charges.

714. The pledge is created by an agreement between the debtor and the creditor. The pledge agreement will be governed by both the general provisions of the General Contracts Law and the more specific provisions of the Pledges Law. However, the Pledges Law may also be considered as a general law, applicable to all kinds of pledges made by agreement, regardless of the particular nature of the property or the provisions of the charge. There are, in addition, other laws which stipulate yet more specific provisions concerning specific kinds of pledges (e.g., the Land Law, 1969, which concerns mortgages on land, the Companies Law, 2000, which deals with securities on corporate property).

§2. The Nature of a Pledge

715. The nature of pledge is defined in section 1(a) of the Pledges Law which provides as follows:

> [a] pledge is a charge on property as a security for an obligation; it entitles the creditor to recoup himself out of the pledged property if the obligation has not been discharged.

716. The pledge institution was created in order to enable the creditor to efficiently secure payback for debts. If the obligation is not fulfilled in due date, the creditor may sell the pledge and collect the debt from its proceeds. Special procedures are provided for the realization of a pledge: instead of applying to the court and afterwards to the Execution Office, the creditor may apply directly to the Chief Execution Officer and the realization will take effect in accordance with the order of the Chief Execution Officer in resemblance to the realization of property attached in execution of a judgment. The pledge entitles the creditor to priority in bankruptcy. The creditor will be entitled to collect his debt from the pledge, and his rights will not be affected by the debtor's bankruptcy.

717. The pledge does not have an independent existence apart from the primary obligation; it is an accessory obligation, made in order to serve the primary one and to enable the creditor to collect the debt. The function of the pledge is similar to that of the guarantee. The definition of pledge as an accessory obligation has various implications concerning its legal status. If, for example, the primary obligation is void, the pledge will also be void, if the primary obligation ceases, the pledge shall terminate. The transfer of the primary obligation will also convey the pledge. In all these cases the legal status of the pledge will depend on the legal status of the primary obligation.

718. In order to enable the creditor to recoup the debt from the pledged property, it is essential that the creditor's right in the pledged property be protected in rem; otherwise the debtor would be able to eliminate the creditor's right by changing the titles to the pledged property. For this reason, the pledge entitles the creditor to a property right in the pledged property. Hence, in holding a pledge the creditor is protected from any changes effectuating the status of the pledged property occurring after the creation of the primary obligation.

719. The Pledges Law provides two principal methods in which a pledge will become effective against other creditors of the debtor. First, the pledged property may be deposited with the creditor or with a bailee on behalf of the creditor. The pledge will be effective upon the deposit thereof and so long as it remains deposited. Second, the pledge may be registered in the Pledges Register Office. However, the pledge shall be effective against a creditor who knew or should have known of the pledge even without registration. In the case of mortgages of land, the mortgage must be registered in the Land Register Office in order to have effect against other creditors. After the pledge has been deposited or registered as aforesaid, the creditor will have a right in rem in the pledged property which will be effective against other creditors of the debtor. Therefore, subject to the 'market overt' rules, even if the debtor transfers ownership in the pledged property to another person, the pledged property will continue to be subordinate to the pledge, and the creditor will be able to realize the pledge in the case of non-fulfilment of the debt.

720. Although the pledge is created by agreement between the debtor and creditor, the power of the parties to stipulate the terms of the agreement according to their will is limited. The first limitation concerns the types of property that may be pledged: where the transfer of ownership in any property is restricted by law or agreement, such property cannot be made the object of a pledge (e.g., social security benefits are non-transferable by law; accordingly, the pledge thereof is impossible). The reason for this provision is clear: the realization of the pledge is performed by the sale and the transfer of ownership in the pledged property. Therefore, where the transfer of ownership is forbidden the creation of a pledge in respect to such property will also be prohibited.

721. Additional restrictions on the freedom of contract of the parties derive from the purpose of the Pledges Law. Certain restrictions exist in order to protect the rights of third parties. The creation of a pledge may effect the rights of third parties, e.g., other creditors of the debtor who lent the debtor money in the belief that he had sufficient unpledged property to cover the debt, as well as other persons who had acquired rights in the pledged property. In order to protect such third parties against the loss that they may sustain because of an unknown pledge, the pledge will be valid only against creditors who knew about it. Accordingly, the law provides two alternative ways of bringing the existence of a pledge to the knowledge of potential creditors: the deposition and the registration. In the absence of deposition or registration the pledge will have no effect against other creditors, unless such creditors knew or should have known of the pledge.

722. Further restrictions are employed in order to protect the interests of the debtor. If the pledged property was deposited with the creditor, the creditor shall not be at liberty to use the pledged property or enjoy the income thereof, unless the debtor has so authorized him in the pledge agreement or at a later stage. Where the debtor has authorized the use or the enjoyment of the pledged property, the creditor shall pay the debtor appropriate consideration unless otherwise agreed. The debtor may redeem the pledge by fulfilling the primary obligation after the period provided for its fulfilment, even if otherwise stipulated in the pledge agreement. The debtor may also redeem the pledge by fulfilling the obligation before the period provided for its fulfilment, unless otherwise stipulated in the pledge agreement. However, in the case of an interest-bearing monetary obligation, the debtor shall be obliged to pay the creditor the interest which would have become due to him up to the time for the fulfilment of the obligation or up to six months after payment, whichever is the earlier date.

723. Section 2(b) of the Pledges Law provides as follows:

> The provisions of this law shall apply to every transaction, however designated, the intention of which is to charge property as security for obligation.

724. The purpose of this provision is to prevent parties from avoiding the application of those provisions in the law intended to protect the debtor and third parties. Hence, the Law shall apply to every agreement which, by its essence and the intention of the parties, is a pledge agreement. The definition of an agreement as a pledge agreement will depend on the true economic and commercial purpose of the agreement, as intended by the parties. A pledge agreement may, for example, be disguised as a hire or sales agreement. However, regardless of the formal label attached to it, certain factors will indicate that the true intention of the parties had been to create a charge on property. In such cases the Pledges Law should apply to the agreement. The agreement may entitle the creditor to certain rights in the debtor's property, such as the right to sell it, to exercise some other control over the transferability of the property, or to hold or use the property – in all such cases it will be possible and appropriate to define the transaction as a pledge. This may also be the case where the debtor ostensibly transfers the ownership in the property to the creditor, yet retains the right to buy the property back from the creditor, or remains in possession of the property. The economic and commercial purpose of the agreement, combined with other evidence concerning the true intention of the parties, will serve as indicators from which the true nature of the transaction as a pledge agreement may be inferred.

§3. RIGHTS AND DUTIES OF THE CREDITOR

725. In consequence of the creation of the pledge agreement, the creditor possesses a number of specific rights and duties. The first right, which derives from the nature of pledge, is the property right in the pledged property. This right enables the creditor to realize the pledged property in order to collect the debt from the resulting proceeds. The property right in the pledged property gives the creditor a preferred position in collecting his debt vis-à-vis other creditors of the debtor.

726. The pledge serves as security not only for the primary obligation but also for interest, expenses and damages payable by the debtor in respect of the obligation, as well as expenses related to the safekeeping and realization of the pledged property. All of these accessory obligations shall be treated in the same manner as the primary obligation covered by the pledge. However, where the extent of the obligation is increased, by agreement between the debtor and the creditor, the pledge shall not serve as security for the additional amount unless the pledge has been increased for that purpose.

727. Where the pledged property is deposited with the creditor, the pledge shall apply also to the income of the pledged property, unless otherwise provided in the pledge agreement. However, the creditor shall not be at liberty to use the pledged property or enjoy the income thereof, unless the debtor has so authorized him in the pledge agreement or subsequently. In that case the creditor shall pay the debtor appropriate consideration for the use in the property or its income. These provisions reflect the difference in legal status, as well as the difference in purpose, between hire and pledge. The pledge is deposited in the creditor in order to secure the debtor's obligation. Unlike the hire, its primary purpose is not to grant the creditor possession and use of the pledged property.

728. The pledge gives the creditor the right to collect the debt by means of the realization of the pledge. However, the giving of a pledge shall not prejudice the creditor's right to collect otherwise than by the realization thereof. The creditor retains the discretion to collect the debt by other legal means. Moreover, if the value of the pledge is inadequate to cover the entire debt, the creditor may employ other legal means in order to collect the balance not discharged by the realization of the pledge.

§4. RIGHTS AND DUTIES OF THE DEBTOR

729. The debtor is under the duty to fulfil the primary obligation. If the primary obligation is not fulfilled at the due date, the creditor may realize the pledge, through the Chief Execution Officer, without applying to the court.

730. As long as the pledge is not realized, the ownership right in the pledged property remains with the debtor. However, the debtor's ownership right is subordinated to the pledge. Every transaction made with regard to the pledged property will be subject to the pledge. Most importantly, the debtor's right to charge the pledged property with an additional pledge is limited: the debtor may charge the pledged property with an additional pledge without obtaining permission from the creditor, but unless provided otherwise in the earlier pledge agreement, an additional creditor shall be unable to recoup himself out of the pledged property until the obligation secured by the earlier pledge has been discharged. Only with the consent of the first creditor may the debtor charge the pledged property with an additional pledge equal or prior in rank to the pledge of that creditor.

731. As long as the primary obligation is fulfilled, or in the case of the debtor's failure to fulfil the primary obligation, as long as the execution proceedings have not been terminated, the debtor retains the ownership right in the property. After the termination of the execution proceedings and the realization of the pledge, any amount received by the creditor will be used to cover the obligation and the balance will be transferred to the debtor. The property right in the pledged property will be conferred from the debtor to the purchaser, and the pledge will cease to exist.

732. The creditor's right of realization is limited: the debtor may redeem the pledge by fulfilling the obligation after the time set for its fulfilment, even if otherwise provided in the agreement.

Chapter 10. Government Contracts

§1. Government as a Contracting Party

733. The State of Israel is a legal personality under private law and conforms to the definition of an incorporated body, i.e., a legal phenomenon, not a person, to which the law attributes rights and duties that are distinguished from the rights and duties of the persons that comprise it. The state has the capacity to acquire rights and duties, to engage in legal transactions and to undertake contractual obligations. The organs through which the state acts are primarily the executive authorities, namely, the cabinet ministers and government departments. The Government of Israel is therefore both an organ and an agent of the state for performing its legal actions.[158]

§2. 'Governmental' and 'Commercial' Contracts of the Government

734. Following certain foreign legal systems, Israeli case law too made a distinction between commercial and governmental contracts of the public authority. The roots of this distinction can be found in a broader distinction within the authority's activities, namely, whether it acts as a government or as a fiscus (private owner of property). As government contracts constitute a type of governmental activity, this distinction was applied to them as well. Consequently, government contracts were described in case law as contracts made by the public authority in the exercise of its public functions.[159] Thus, for example, contracts that included an obligation not to confiscate land, to prefer a particular importer or producer, to grant a licence, to allocate foreign currency, or similar commitments regarding the public authority's statutory powers, were all classified as governmental.[160] Government contracts that did not include such obligations were considered commercial.

735. The distinction between commercial and governmental contracts of the government should be rejected, at both the practical and the theoretical levels. The application of the distinction between governmental and commercial administrative contracts seems to be almost impossible, since contracts made between the government and private citizens are often difficult to classify. Indeed, close examination of

158. This power is founded in the residual powers of the Government, as provided in s. 32 of Basic Law: The Government, 22 LSI 257. The State Property Law, 1951, (5 LSI 45) recognizes the State of Israel as the owner of property and as having the power to acquire and transfer property, and it also establishes the Government's status as an organ acting in the name of the State in all transactions related to State property.

159. *Balaban v. Municipality of Tel Aviv* (1952) 6 PD 257; *Miller v. Minister of Transport* (1961) 15 PD1989, 2005.

160. *Miller, ibid.*; *Electra (Israel) Inc. v. Minister of Commerce and Industry* (1968) 22(2) PD 551.

the instances in which the distinction between governmental and commercial contracts has been applied by the courts in Israel would reveal these decisions are inconsistent and often contradictory.[161]

736. No distinction should be made between governmental and commercial contracts. Every government contract contains and combines the two aspects, governmental and commercial, the first stemming from the character of the contracting party and the second from the nature of the contract itself. Indeed, there are government contracts in which the first aspect is more prominent, while in others the second is emphasized, but this alone does not justify or allow for the distinction considered above. By its very nature, every government contract entails public and private, governmental and commercial aspects, its very description as a government contract bearing consequences with regard to both the applicable law and the jurisdiction of the court. These consequences are not dependent on any internal classification of government contracts.

§3. The Law of Government Contracts

737. Comprising a dual personality, government contracts are subject *a priori* and simultaneously to two systems of law: contract law and public law. Contract law applies due to the nature of the legal act under discussion (a contract), while public law applies as a result of the nature of the contracting party (the government). Each time a governmental body binds itself by a contract, its action will be examined in a dual perspective: the validity of its public powers will be determined in accordance with public law, while the validity of the contract, the rights and duties of the parties, the formation and the termination of the contract, will be referred to private law.

738. Contract law ought to apply to government contracts. This proposition follows from the basic constitutional principle of the rule of law and primarily from its substantive aspect which strives for the equality of the state and its citizens before the law. This approach is not only just but also efficient, in encouraging contracting with the government.

739. Since a government contract is classified as a contract, and therefore subject to the provisions of contract law, all rights and duties of the state are determined in accordance to the General Contracts Law. The General Contracts Law

161. For example, the issuance of an import licence (in effect granting a monopoly) by a public authority was described as 'a contract of clear commercial nature' (*Meichal Umassah Shipping Co. Ltd. v. Minister of Finance* (1957) 11 PD 1490, 1511), whereas the issuance or denial of import licences in another case was described as 'a clear governmental act' (*Rehovot Packing House v. Minister of Agriculture* (1962) 16 PD 20, 29); housing contracts between the government and the potential occupants were considered commercial contracts not warranting the intervention of the High Court of Justice (*Irgun HaMishtaknim v. Minister of Labour* (1953) 7(2) PD 922), whereas the actual construction of the governmental housing project was classified as a governmental act (*Van Mirop v. Director of Housing Department* (1957) 11 PD 659).

does not distinguish between types of contracting parties and should therefore make no distinction between contracts made between private citizens and government contracts.[162] The State and citizen should be subject to the same legal regime with regard to the formation of a contract and its performance, and all rights and duties should be determined according to the General Contracts Law.

740. A contract is only one recourse of many through which the government may materialize its economic needs. Other means include regulations, confiscation and by-laws. However, when the government chooses to make a contract, it removes its governmental cloak and cannot then be distinguished from a private citizen acting as a contracting party. This choice places the government, by virtue of its own free will, in the contractual framework.

741. In practice, the Israeli Supreme Court has applied the entire law of contract, its principles, rules and minute details to government contracts.[163] This application was not always explained or even consciously considered, but on almost every occasion in which a government contract was discussed, the application of the law of contract was considered self-evident.

742. Special laws apply to government contracts, in conjunction with private law. The application of these laws results from the fact that one of the parties to a government contract is a public authority. Therefore, these laws are derived from the law that provides the norms for the government's activity, namely public law.

743. Considering the fact that every government contract involves some kind of legal activity of the government, the government is therefore obligated, as a trustee of the public, to act in a fair, honest and indiscriminate manner in all the various contractual stages. The government must act with the same degree of fairness and good faith, when operating in the sphere of public or private law. Public law is therefore the source of the government's duties as a party to a government contract. Public law also constitutes the source of the government's substantive and procedural immunity and privileges.

---

162. However, in a recent decision, two judges of the Supreme Court did try to classify contracts into categories and attach different principles of contract interpretation to government contracts. Discussed above at paras 41–42.

163. The general law of contract was applied in the pre-contractual stages of a government contract, such as the negotiations towards the formation of the contract (e.g., *Burkan v. Minister of Finance* (1978) 32(2) PD 800) as well as at the stage of formation of contractual intent (*Reis v. Israel Land Authority* (1978) 32(2) PD 617). Government contracts were interpreted according to the normal rules of contract interpretation (*State of Israel v. Maoz* (1976) 30(3) PD 748). The laws of defects in formation (*Cohen v. Minister of Defence* (1980) 34(2) PD 465), as well as the law regarding breach of contract (*State of Israel v. 'Li-Or'* (1969) 23(1) PD 436) and illegality (*ibid.*; *Burger v. State of Israel* (1965) 19(2) PD 228), were also applied to government contracts. The Supreme Court even applied to such contracts the general principle of freedom of contract, embodied today in s. 24 of the General Contracts Law ('even' because obviously the public authority's freedom of contract is narrower than that of the individual).

744. The intrinsic nature of government contracts is contract law, this law applying to government contracts in conjunction with the 'personal law' of the contracting parties: the 'personal law' of the government being public law.

745. A question arises as to the possible outcome in a case of conflict between the two systems of law, private and public, that apply concurrently to a government contract. The solution suggested here is simple. The rules of public law that apply to government contracts are *lex specialis* that prevails over the General Contracts Law whenever the two clash: *lex specialis derogat lex generalis.* Technically speaking, there is no difference between the application of public law to government contracts and the application of any other special law to any other contract. As in the case of a typical contract of sale, where the General Contracts Law applies together with laws of sale, laws derived from public law apply to government contracts concurrently with the general laws of contract. This rule helps to explain the privileges as well as the additional duties of the government as a party to a contract. In a case of conflict between the privileges and duties of the government and the General Contracts Law, these rights and duties take priority over the General Contracts Law.

§4. Public Tenders

746. The Israeli legislator applied the public tender system to the central administration in 1992. Until then, unlike municipal bodies, which are obligated by law to issue public tenders prior to entering into contracts,[164] the State of Israel and its authorities were not required by law to initiate the contracting process through public tenders.[165] Nevertheless, in practice, the public tender system was applied to many government transactions by virtue of governmental regulations, primarily those issued by the General Registrar in the Ministry of Finance. These regulations, establishing procedures for procurement by the state authorities via public tenders, express government policy and were therefore considered internal directives of the administration. As such, they were usually binding, but the administration could deviate from them when this was justified.

747. Thus, in most cases a government contract was preceded by a tender. Public authorities often conducted tenders on their own accord, without being governed or dictated by any duty (not even a duty resulting from internal directives). The judicial tendency was more lenient towards such voluntary tenders. These were annulled only when the defects in their execution caused fundamental conflicts with the principles of public tender law developed by the Israeli High Court of Justice, particularly the principle of equality and the requirement of fair competition.

---

164. *See, e.g.*, for municipalities, s. 197 of the Municipalities Ordinance (New Version), 1964, 1 LSI (N.V.) 247.
165. Employment contracts constitute an exception – these must be preceded by tenders. *See* s. 19 of the State Service (Appointments) Law, 1959 13 LSI 203.

748. The Public Tenders Law, 1992, imposed the duty of public tenders on the State of Israel, as well as on other statutory incorporated bodies and on all government corporations. This duty applies to all procurement contracts, a broad category that includes land transactions as well as contracts for services. The Public Tenders Law, 1992, grants the Minister of Finance a wide authority to exempt certain transactions from the duty of tender. This authority was utilized in the Public Tenders Regulations, 1992, where no less than thirty-one categories of transactions were exempted from the duty of public tender.

749. As in the case of government contracts, two systems of law concurrently apply to public tenders – contract law and public law. This application of both systems to public tenders has been termed by the Israeli Supreme Court a 'normative duality'.[166] Public tenders can thus be described and analysed in the context of both private and public law. From a private law perspective, a public tender can be described as a stage in the history of a government contract, and as part of the pre-contractual negotiations. From a public law perspective, a public tender can be described as a stage in the history of a government contract, as part of the pre-contractual negotiations and as part of the government's activity.

750. Israeli public tender law was developed mainly by decisions of the High Court of Justice, while exercising its judicial control over administrative action. The law of public tenders of the government can be located in two subdivisions of laws: first, in the Public Tenders Law, 1992 and second, in the rules of public law, applying the basic principles of government activity, to tenders. The application of public law to tenders results from the fact that the offeror of the tender is a public authority. This is an example of the authority bearing its 'personal' law, namely public law, in all its activities.

751. Application of public law to tenders can create situations alien to the basic principle of contract law, namely freedom of contract. These include situations in which the authority is required to contract with a particular party or situations in which its contract will be annulled because of reasons rooted in public law, such as discrimination or acting beyond authority (*ultra vires*).

752. The public authority's use of a tender in making a contract can also be described in contract law terminology. In contractual terms, a tender is not an offer that can become a contract by virtue of the mere acceptance of the participating party. A tender is only an invitation to treat, an earlier stage – both logically and chronologically – in the crystallization of the contracting party's will.[167] Each of the offers that are received in response to the tender constitute an 'offer', as defined in section 2 of the General Contracts Law. The authority's decision to contract with one applicant constitutes an acceptance of the offer, and a government contract is thus effectuated. As the elements of consent and definiteness, both required under

166. Primarily by Justice Barak, in numerous decisions. For example, *Plonit Company v. Minister of Defence* (1980) 34(3) PD 706, 716; *Hasam Defence Systems v. Israel Police* (1983) 37(1) PD 473.
167. Discussed above at paras 101–102.

Israeli contract law to create an offer,[168] are not required in a tender, a tender may be qualified. The issuer of the tender can reserve the option to reject all offers, or to accept only those offers he prefers. From a contractual point of view, every qualification in the tender will be regarded as legitimate.

753. The government contract following the tender is created when the public authority accepts one of the offers. Thereafter the tender is merged into the contract, thereby binding the parties. The public authority cannot effectively annul the tender (which does not exist anymore as such), and none of the contracting parties can rescind without being considered in breach of contract.

754. By demanding parties to the pre-contractual negotiations to act in good faith, section 12 of the General Contracts Law incorporates such negotiations into the legitimate area of contract law.[169] The negotiations towards a government contract start with the publication of a tender. The good faith provision of section 12 therefore applies to the publication of the tender, the drafting of its terms, the conduct of the parties in accordance with it, the reception and consideration of offers and the choice of one of them. Indeed, the Supreme Court, by viewing the tender proceedings as pre-contractual negotiations, has applied the good faith provision to public tenders on a number of opportunities.[170]

755. Section 12 provides an additional theoretical basis for the public authority's duty to act honestly and fairly in the public tender proceedings, yet it does not abolish other sources applying to these proceedings, derived from public law.

756. The requirement of section 12 (as well as section 39, regarding good faith in the performance of a contract) is twofold. On the one hand, it is a cumulative requirement to the normal obligations. On the other hand, it is a minimal and moderating requirement, allowing, in certain cases, a deviation from the perfect performance of the obligation, provided the performance and deviation were executed in good faith.

757. Applying this second aspect of the good faith provision to the domain of tenders provides a dogmatic-analytical basis for the Supreme Court's longstanding tendency as to not annul a tender merely due to minor, non-fundamental defects in its proceedings. The rule providing that a public tender should be upheld in spite of formal or technical defects, when these did not cause injustice, conforms to the good faith principle and its moderating aspect.

758. Placing public tenders within the framework of private law also enables awarding damages to the injured party, a remedy which is rare in public law. The

168. Discussed above at paras 91 et seq.
169. Discussed above at paras 143 et seq.
170. *See*, e.g., *Ben Haim v. Israel Land Authority* (1975) 30(1) PD 412, 413; *Maior Co. v. Netivei Ayalon Co.* (1981) 35(3) PD 596, 601.

usual remedies with regard to tenders range from declaring the tender void to annulment of the authority's decision and obligating it to reconsider the offers. However, viewing public tenders as part of the pre-contractual negotiations paves the way for the award of negative, reliance damages, as provided for in section 12(b).[171]

171. Discussed above at paras 166–171.

Chapter 11. Quasi-Contracts: Unjust Enrichment

759. Prior to 1979 principles relating to restitution on the grounds of unjust enrichment were imported from English law. Hence, English law – as applied by the Israeli courts – became the primary source of the law of quasi-contracts and of equitable principles designed to prevent unjust enrichment in a number of different contexts. However, during this period the Israeli Supreme Court often adopted – as for example in the case of developments relating to restitution of a payment made as a result of a mistake of law – an independent stance which deviated from English decisions. The liberal approach of the Supreme Court reflected the view that the categories upon which restitution may be granted are open, and was instrumental in leading to the gradual recognition of a general principle of restitution on the grounds of unjust enrichment.

760. In 1979 the Israeli legislator stepped in and enacted a statute concerning unjust enrichment, designed to regulate the subject as a whole: the Unjust Enrichment Law, 1979 (hereinafter: the Law).[172] The Law was one of well over a dozen statutes enacted during the previous decades in the area of civil law, in an effort to replace and modernize the law of the Ottoman and Mandatory periods.[173] The declared purpose of the Law is to cover the wide area known in English law as 'quasi-contract' and in American law simply as 'restitution', and to provide solutions to legal problems and issues in relation to which traditional contract, tort and property law are silent. Like some of the legislations of this period, the Law was also influenced by principles taken from Jewish law. In typical fashion, the statute is short, comprising several sweeping provisions expressing broadly formulated, general principles and leaving much scope for the exercise of judicial discretion. The provisions of the law apply also to the State.

761. The pivotal provisions of the Law are stipulated in section 1, which provides:

(a) Where a person obtains any property, service or other benefits from another person without legal cause (the two persons hereinafter respectively referred to as 'the beneficiary' and 'the benefactor'), the beneficiary shall make restitution to the benefactor, and if restitution in kind is impossible or unreasonable shall pay him the value of the benefit.
(b) It shall be immaterial whether the benefit was obtained through an act of the beneficiary or an act of the benefactor or in any other way.

762. Under section 2 of the Law the court is given discretion to exempt the beneficiary from the whole or part of the duty of restitution pursuant to section 1 if it considers that the receipt of the benefit did not involve a loss to the benefactor or that other circumstances render restitution unjust. Section 3 of the Law enables the

172. Discussed above at paras 50–56.
173. Discussed above at paras 15–21.

beneficiary, in making restitution, to deduct what he has reasonably expended or undertaken to expend or invested in order to obtain the benefit.

763. The Law contains a special provision concerning a situation in which one person pays another person's debt without being under a duty towards him to do so. In such circumstances, the person paying the debt will not be entitled to restitution for the amount paid if the debtor has any reasonable cause to object to the payment of the whole or part of the debt (section 4).

764. Section 5 of the Law makes provision for the indemnification and compensation of a person who, without being under an obligation to do so, reasonably and in good faith acts to protect another person's interest – whether it be the other person's life, physical integrity, health, honour or property – and in that connection incurs or undertakes to incur any expenses, or suffers damage to his property.

765. Since its enactment, the Law has had a pervasive influence on Israeli law. A landmark decision which aptly illustrates the manner in which the broad principles of the Law have been applied to situations previously governed exclusively by more traditional doctrines, thereby giving rise to novel legal responses, is that of *Adras Construction Co. Ltd. v. Harlow & Jones G.M.B.H.*[174]

766. In that case the Supreme Court first considered the question whether, in view of section 6(a) of the Law, the Law can apply along and side by side with a contract between the parties. Section 6(a) of the Law provides as follows: 'The provisions of this law shall apply where no other law contains special provisions as to the matter in question and no agreement between the parties provides otherwise.' The answer to that question was in the affirmative. The Supreme Court decided that section 6(a) did not bar the application of the Law, despite the contractual relation between the parties.

767. Having decided that the Law can apply also in a context of contractual relations, the Supreme Court considered the application of section 1 of the Law to the facts of the case. It was decided that the buyer, the injured party, was entitled to disgorgement of any benefit gained by the seller as a result of selling the goods to a third party.

174. *Adras, supra* note 12. A detailed English summary of the case can be found in (1990) 24 Is. L.R. 150.

Selected Bibliography

Books

Shalev, G. & Zemach, E, *The Law of Contracts*. 4th ed., Isreal: Din, 2019.
Shalev, G. & Adar, Y. *The Law of Contracts – Remedies for Breach: Towards Codification of Israeli Civil Law*. Isreal: Din, 2009.
Shalev, G. *The Law of Public Procurement.* Isreal: Din, 1999.

Legislation

LSI – Laws of the State of Israel (Official translation of Israeli statutes).

Cases

PD – 'Piskei Din' – Judgments of Israeli Supreme Court.

Selected Bibliography

Index

The numbers here refer to paragraph numbers.

Index

www.ingramcontent.com/pod-product-compliance
Lightning Source LLC
Chambersburg PA
CBHW071447230926
51846CB00001B/378
9789403529905